D0272545

Clever Girl

Also by Brian Thompson

Keeping Mum
A Monkey Among Crocodiles
Imperial Vanities
The Nightmare of a Victorian Bestseller
Devastating Eden

Clever Girl

A SENTIMENTAL EDUCATION

Brian Thompson

ATLANTIC BOOKS
LONDON

First published in Great Britain in 2007 by Atlantic Books,
an imprint of Grove Atlantic Ltd.

Copyright © Brian Thompson 2006

The moral right of Brian Thompson to be identified as
the author of this work has been asserted in accordance with
the Copyright, Designs and Patents Act of 1988.

1 3 5 7 9 8 6 4 2

A CIP catalogue record for this book is available from
the British Library.

ISBN: 978 1 84354 544 6

Designed and typeset by Patty Rennie Production
Printed in Great Britain

Atlantic Books
An imprint of Grove Atlantic Ltd
Ormond House
26–27 Boswell Street
London WC1N 3JZ

For Shirley

Clever Girl

Chapter One

IN 1952, MY FATHER BERT CAME HOME ON A weekend visit to Cambridge and, as they used to say in those days, issued a brief communiqué. In a month's time we would all be living in Waltham Cross. For my mother, myself and my six-year-old brother Neil, the news came as the equivalent of being told that the Russians were storming ashore at Margate or that he, finally tiring of us, had taken up the life of the circus.

His intentions were quite the opposite. This was to be a grand reunion of a family that had not lived together on a daily basis since 1940, during which time the language of love had grown decidedly rusty. Since the end of the war my father had lived and worked in London, leaving us to slog it out in Cambridge. It was a solution to his sense of outrage at my mother's romantic adventures with the USAAF Eighth Air Force, though he might have been surprised at how little she seemed to remember those giddy days. In place of all the confusion she had caused was now a resigned indifference.

1

She drooped. Going with Yanks, as everybody described it in the 1940s, had at least given her something to look forward to in a dull week. When the Americans left, they took her sense of self-worth with them.

Peace had improved my father's standing greatly. Only a month or so before the shattering news of our departure from Cambridge, he had come home on a similarly brief visit and boasted that he was now on a salary of £1,000 a year. We were in the kitchen eating salad when he made the announcement, at which I let it be known that anyone who earned £20 a week was surely acting against the interests of those worse off. Such a person was, considered in the right light, an enemy of the people.

'How's that?' he asked. Laying down his knife and fork, he leaned across the table and cuffed me to the floor, along with the salad bowl and a jar of pickled onions.

'You,' he pointed out, 'have never earned a penny in your life.'

'That doesn't make me wrong,' I shouted from the lino.

'It doesn't give you a right to an opinion at all. When I was your age—'

'Oh, here we go!' my mother cried. 'Get the fiddles out.'

'Oh yes, you! You stick up for him, why don't you?'

He opened the back door and walked out into the wreck of a garden that had once been his dream of contentment. My mother poured a cup of tea and indicated that I should take it out to him. He was standing in the centre of the shaggy lawn, hands plunged into pockets.

'I've worked damned hard since I left the RAF. That counts for nothing, apparently.'

It was not in my father's nature to reveal his deeper feelings – that way lay weakness and (since his enemy was the whole world) danger. But there was something raw in this remark that made me wince. He took the tea and turned his back. I can see now that he was trying to avoid having to face down a lath of a boy, dressed in jeans and the hated emblem of American occupation, a white GI-issue T-shirt. We were standing in exactly the same place as we had been when, twelve years earlier, he came home to tell us he had volunteered for RAF aircrew.

'You deserved a bloody good clout,' he muttered.

It was the first time he had ever hit me in real anger, whereas my mother's most recent exasperation with family life had led her to throw a bread-knife at me: it missed its mark but dislodged the electric iron on a shelf above my head. I had been laid out cold for ten minutes, which, in those more innocent days, seemed no time at all, neither to her nor to me. 'Now look what you've done,' she said when I came round.

The clout my father gave me had actually knocked, if not sense, then a touch of realism into me. I was already taller than he was and it was very unlikely that, at any time of my future life, I would be wearing braces to hold up my trousers, as he did. His hair was beginning to thin and his pale eyes were tinged with yellow. We were strangers to each other, of course, as unlike as chalk and cheese – but that was something I had understood a long, long time ago. In this particular instance the story was about him. I realised with a horrible admission of guilt that I was a sorry disappointment to all he held dear.

'You don't feel ashamed?' he asked, as if reading my mind.

'About what?' I havered.

He shrugged.

'Have it your way. I would want more from life than making up the numbers.'

It was code but I knew what he meant. At that time the average wage was £4 a week. Before the war he had been a telephone linesman, hanging from poles by a leather strap. And, his cocky stubbornness seemed to be saying, look at me now. Staying on at school in the sixth form, reading a load of silly bloody books, did not count. While he was wrestling the tiller as the boat struggled to clear the bar in a sky filled with spume, I was on the shore, wringing my hands like a herring girl.

Buying a house was an outward sign of Bert's new status and it may also have been a gesture of reparation. If that were so, it failed spectacularly. We were all dumbfounded. We had no idea where Waltham Cross was. Nor could he furnish any idea of what the new place looked like.

'What does any house look like?' he scoffed.

'Well, how many bedrooms does it have?'

'Three,' he said uncertainly. 'Two and a bit, anyway. It's a house.'

'A semi?'

'A terrace.'

He pointed his cigarette at me.

'Get yourself up the council offices or wherever you have to go and find yourself a school locally.'

'Is that all there is to it?'

'How do I know? Use your loaf.'

'But I'm halfway through the sixth-form syllabus here.'

'What's that got to do with it?'

My mother returned to the more pressing question.

'I will ask you once again,' she said with her most dangerous silky emphasis, 'where is this effing dump?'

My interview with the Education Department took place with an official so evidently new to the job that I felt at an immediate advantage. I was facing a plump young graduate, seemingly straight from the bath, with delicate fair hair and an almost round face. He wore a stiff suit and played nervously with his shirt cuffs. Like me, he had some difficulty in finding Waltham Cross, which he placed first in Essex, then in Middlesex, and finally in Hertfordshire.

'There's a grammar school in Cheshunt. It's co-educational. There's an all-boys' school in Hertford.'

'Where's that?'

'Yes, where can it be?' he sneered.

'I'd prefer Hertford.'

'Oh, you'd prefer it! And is your preference what we might call an informed one?'

'I'll take it,' I insisted.

The education officer made more play of shooting his cuffs and reached for his tea. Much of it was in the saucer. There was a clock above his head that marked the seconds with a grudging clunk. We were at an impasse.

'What about your parents? Don't they have an opinion on the matter?'

'They are mentally unstable and in no position to judge.'

'They are both mentally unstable?'

'They have driven each other barmy,' I explained.

When I walked out of the Education Offices, my girl-friend Figgie was leaning against a wall, looking martyred. She had sneaked out from the place where she worked and greeted me as though I had just signed up for a ten-year hitch with the Foreign Legion.

'How are we ever going to stay together now?' she wailed, her eyes great pools of tears. We embraced in utter helplessness. The wasting disease that afflicts first love had cast its shadow. We were about to be doomed by long distance.

In 1290, King Edward I's wife, Eleanor of Castile, died in Lincolnshire. The body was carried to London by stages and at every resting place the clergy who accompanied it persuaded local notables to erect a memorial cross. Three of these survive, one of them on the west bank of the River Lee at a place called Waltham. Who is to say what the locals made of it when it was first installed? Nowadays it was the marker point for a trolley bus turn-round and a boundary stone for the activities of the Metropolitan Police. London lay eleven miles away. Where once the cortège had passed through silent and untenanted forests there were now huge tracts of housing, factories, shopping arcades and trading estates. Even in urban landscapes there are more trees than imagination provides but this part of north London has little natural beauty left in it. In the 1950s it was drear.

It was not history that had tugged my father's sleeve and drawn his attention to the Cross, as the locals called it, but something much more practical. From six in the morning, stopping trains from Cambridge scooped up commuters and delivered them to the sooty and fish-smelling terminus at Liverpool Street. There these clerks and managers, typists and secretaries streamed off the platform and tramped up a steep concourse before dispersing to banks and offices in London Wall, Bishopsgate and beyond. In the evening, they made the return journey covered in the dust and grime of the capital.

In summer months, their passage home was made in mocking sunshine, with just enough of the day left over after supper to mow the lawn or water the flower-beds. When the nights grew shorter they marched away from the station in long files, breasting the dark like defeated soldiers. Emptied of passengers, the trains rumbled on to Cambridge, bearing hundreds of copies of the *Evening Standard*, empty cigarette packets, mislaid gloves, love letters, scarves and umbrellas.

Our place in the shapeless dormitory that Waltham had become since medieval cows scratched their rumps against Queen Eleanor's Cross was on an estate of postwar housing drabbling to the railway line. The street names were unimaginative and the design of each house identically stark. Twenty years earlier, this parcel of land had been given over to market gardening and whereas in Cambridge we had famously dug chalk, now the spade turned up broken glass and bits of flower-pot. My father had bought a stake in this paradise at the controlled price of £1,650, a figure that stays in the mind because so often repeated.

For as long as she had been living in one of Europe's premier university towns my mother never tired of disparaging what she called 'the Swedes' who lived there and serviced its colleges. Waltham Cross and its denizens outraged her. There were no high fences in Eastfield Road to shield us from our neighbours, or behind which we could hide ourselves. Shortly after arriving, she looked out of the bedroom window and discovered Alf from next door peeing peaceably against the wall of his coal bunker. It did not help that he was wearing his Parachute Regiment beret on the back of his head and holding a garden fork in his free hand.

The houses were ridiculously small. When the four of us sat at table it was impossible to open the drawers to the new sideboard. We carried on the working-class tradition of making the front room the best room; the three-piece suite we had brought with us from Cambridge crouched there like a family of caged gorillas. There were no welcoming hearths. In each of the ground-floor rooms was a two-bar electric fire fitted flush to the wall. In cold weather, in addition to the smell of convected dust came the sharp and warning tang of wood varnish heated to flashpoint.

Only a year earlier, in 1951, my father and I had wandered around the Festival of Britain admiring (or not) the best of British design. The house in Eastfield Road pre-dated this promised future. We were living in Gimcrack Alley.

'You'll live here and like it,' Bert snapped. 'These houses will be like gold dust in a few years, once the controls come off.'

'If they haven't fallen down by then,' my mother persisted. She pointed to my brother. 'Mind how you go banging down the lav seat. You could end up in the garden with your trousers round your ankles.'

Neil was not the chortling kind but he gave her instead his slow-burning smile. At mealtimes he was given the chair against the wall and then had the table jammed against his stomach. He never complained. There was no running about to be had anywhere in the house, a loss he compensated for by tumbling down the stairs each morning like a runaway piano.

From wishing to be Robert Mitchum myself, I had been

forced to accept that my brother was as close as anyone in our family would get to that laconic genius. One day I had caught him standing on the cinder path that ran along the back gardens, squinting down the barrel of a Brussels sprout stalk at Jap snipers holed up in the tangle of weeds and brambles beyond.

'Come and get it, little yellow-bellies,' he piped.

In this new life, my father walked to the station every day with selected cronies, all adepts of the *Daily Telegraph* crossword and the homelier parts of the Home Service. For the balance of the journey up to town, they had good old British exasperation to pass the time. The trains were filthy (that's nationalisation for you); the weather was awful (blame the Russians, why not?); you could not find a decent pair of shoes locally to save your life. As for doctors, take what happened to Tarbutt, who used to travel up with them. He complained of a slight dizzy spell on the way home one night and three days later was stretched out in Enfield Chase Hospital, dead as a doorknocker. Tarbutt, the bank messenger whose son was presently dug in on the side of a mountain in Korea, listening to Chinese bugles in the valley below.

There was also – at any rate in my father's case – suppressed sexual delirium on these commuting journeys. Seats were kept in his compartment for slow, shy girls who worked in City offices and had interesting lives. Their boyfriends took them to motor-racing circuits or dance halls where the beat was lively. Their mothers plotted marriage and went to sleep with the tinnitus of wedding bells ringing in their ears. In due course, these clerks and typists removed their gloves to show a tiny diamond engagement ring. After perhaps another year, they took their farewells of the commuter club and married. Their places in the compartment were taken by others, whose lovebites and cotton cardigans, fake pearls and court shoes were examined hungrily by the man in the corner seat, my father.

Not every family had a commuter in it. Alf next door to us was a motor mechanic at a local garage. On the other side was the retired and largely mute Mr Sanderson, who had spent his working life potting on plants at a nursery. The middle class of society, as represented by teachers, doctors, managers, shopkeepers and the like, was absent.

It did not take long to realise that the general mood in the street was brisker and cannier than it had been in Cambridge. The accents were those of London and there was a premium on insider information.

'You say you're looking for a new bath? If you were prepared to go as far as Bruce Grove, my brother-in-law's got half a dozen tucked away in his shed. He drinks at the Feathers. Big bloke, can't miss him. Ask for Dave.'

Early on, from a source like this, my father bought a venerable woodworking lathe. Once he had told a gardening neighbour that he was interested in such a thing, his bluff was called and the lathe was delivered late one night by a ratty man in overalls.

'It's a bit hooky,' he explained, once he had pocketed the notes that Bert passed across. This put the new owner in something of a dilemma. The King had placed his trust in my father, not once but twice. How to explain that to a man with a star tattooed on the back of each hand?

'Only kidding. It's been in our family for generations,' the thief amended cheerfully. 'Anything else you want, talk to Sid and he'll give me a bell.'

But I could tell that he was on the back foot. My father's RAFA tie (or maybe it was the pipe and the fawn cardigan with buttons shaped like footballs) seemed to throw him. He made up for his discomfiture by being excessively polite to my mother, going so far as to wash a cup and saucer at the sink before leaving.

'And now half the bloody crooks in north London know where we live,' she exulted when the man left.

'I can look after myself,' Bert said uneasily. All the same, the lathe went into the toolshed and was wrapped in a coal sack that Neil had found in the roadway. There it stayed until the heat was off.

When I had my interview at the Education Offices in Cambridge I had no idea where Hertford was, any more than I did the location of Truro or Berwick-on-Tweed. This was information easily supplied locally: my new school was a forty-minute bus ride away to the north. I was the furthest flung of its students – the county boundary lay only a few hundred yards from our house, where Middlesex pressed its feral snout. Essex was even closer, a mere fifty yards away on the other side of the railway line. There was nothing to see of it except fields scabby with dock and the occasional rusting water tank.

Standing at the bus stop the first time I took the journey to school, I was the only youth in the queue. Hordes of younger children in brown uniform lallygagged past me on their way to Cheshunt Grammar School. I was accidentally different; they had satchels and briefcases. I stood there with my hands in my pockets, gazing down at what were called in those days brothel-creepers – brown shoes with massive crêpe soles. My footwear had gone unnoticed in Cambridge but I was beginning to wonder whether it would pass muster at this new place. To kill time waiting for the green double-decker, I rolled a cig and recombed my hair.

A little beyond Cheshunt, a plumply confident boy clattered upstairs wearing a blazer with the school crest. Though he was no older than me, his chin was glazed an improbable blue. One by one his acolytes joined him and he began presiding over a boisterous court. His name was John Tydeman and in later life he went on to become a distinguished radio producer and BBC administrator. It was bred in the bone: Tydeman had a joshing side to him and a gift for orchestrating conversation that had me slouching in my seat, sullen and wreathed in the smoke from a Nosegay roll-up. Once or twice he caught my eye. His smile was a perfect mixture of derision and warmth. As we drew near Hertford he came to join me.

'Are you by any chance the Cambridge prodigy?'

'What's that supposed to mean?'

But Tydeman had manners. He walked me through the town to our destination, a foundation grammar school created a year after Shakespeare's death. Housed since 1930 in a handsome brick building approached by rising lawns, it exuded, as I saw it, class. Bunt, the headmaster, to whom I presented myself, was a gangling parsonical figure who pumped my hand vigorously in the lobby of the school, where we were overlooked by a portrait of the founder, Richard Hale. If Dr Bunt's eyes did flicker briefly to my brothel-creepers, he made no mention of them.

'You know, that dreadful old fraud Harold Clunn described Waltham Cross, even as late as 1932, as a little market town, a description that I imagine must come as a surprise to you. But Trollope lived there very well on £800 a year and, I think, wrote the Barsetshire novels – or did he? – Yes, I think he did – oh look, there's Dr Wilkinson! He's the man you need to see.'

Waiting to one side was the senior English master, smiling his crooked smile. Andrew Wilkinson was such a teacher as I had not previously met: calm, good-natured, effortlessly scholarly and, as it was to prove, a brilliant educator. His voice had a pleasant rural burr and he had the habit of cocking his head to one side when speaking, as if exchanging intimacies with you in some tavern snug. He was young, he was creative (he had recently made a film of 'The Pardoner's Tale' with amateur actors) and above all he could read me like a book. We went to sit in an empty classroom to discuss how to adapt what little I knew to what I was to study. There were many longueurs.

'Have you read any modern poets, for example?'

'No.'

'What do you think about the whole idea of modernity?'

'Do you like jazz?' I countered.

'That might be a way of getting to the question. Do you think you could write me a little piece saying what people mean when they talk about modern jazz? What they're trying to indicate by the adjective?'

He had me hooked. A week later, he suggested that I drop Latin, which was one of my three A-levels, and study English and French at the slightly more exalted scholarship level.

'If you think so.'

'No,' he corrected gently. 'It has to be your decision. Tydeman tells me you are reading Pound.'

'Is that good or bad?'

He laughed.

'Read whatever you can get your hands on. Both in French and English. And don't believe absolutely everything John Tydeman says.'

He paused at the door.

'You could try to catch up in history and take that as a third subject.'

I shook my head. Ezra Pound, father of modernity and reckless scholar, suited me just fine. I could hardly understand a word of what he wrote but that too was a beckoning. I imagined him to be a few years older than me (and not a raddled and ignominious wreck of sixty-seven) and knowing about the world in a way that was a poke in the eye with a sharp stick to all at Eastfield Road. Tydeman had lent me his copy of *The Pisan Cantos* and it filled my heart with joy to see the look of incredulity on my father's face as he read a few lines before flinging the book down.

Hertford Grammar School, or more specifically Andrew Wilkinson and Ray Venner (who taught me French with a good-natured savagery fuelled by generous lunchtime draughts of McMullen's Bitter), turned me from a consumer of education into a participant. The little victories of sixth-form life, like occasionally saying on paper exactly what one meant, were the point and purpose of that long druggy ride through rural south Hertfordshire and the journey home.

'You've changed,' my mother said.

'It happens every morning. Soon as I walk out of this door.'

It was a cruel and unnecessary thing to say.

*

The best judge of how much I had changed was Figgie. I went back to Cambridge a few times to see her and we spent our days together in greasy-spoon cafés and cinemas. She told me about Mr Kitto, the office manager at work, and Irene in accounts; I told her about Blake seeing angels roosting in the trees.

'What a snob you are,' she retorted as we said goodbye on the London platform. It was a Sunday night, with shadows like coal dust and the clank of shunting in unseen marshalling yards. What few staff there were sloped about with brooms and buckets or ducked in and out of little offices.

'You don't really mean that.'

'It's like Ian says, you're still only a schoolboy.'

'Who's Ian?' I asked, feeling my heart plummet.

'Someone I know,' Figgie muttered.

The white of her blouse shone like magnolia, her high heels brought her up almost to my height. We stood there staring at each other, each close to tears.

'I love you,' I said.

She turned and ran. When the train came, I found an empty compartment and punched clouds of dust from the cushions, maddened by grief. Only six months ago I would have leaped from the train, found my way back to her house and shouted up at the bedroom windows. I would have door-stepped her place of work, caught up with her as she walked out of the Regal Cinema with Ian and punched his lights out (or be killed in the attempt). But she was right: only a little educational encouragement had turned me from a wolf in the forest to a half-formed swot. I raged around the railway carriage trying to rediscover my fur and fangs.

Tydeman was sympathetic. 'Isn't education supposed to subvert who you were before you started out on it?'

'What do you want to do with your life?'

'Go to Cambridge, I think. Then Italy. Read. Collect interesting people.' He giggled. 'Tall willowy people. Wilkinson thinks you are something special, by the way.'

The bus growled its way up the hill.

'What are your parents like?' I asked, shifting the ground a little.

'Dreadful question!' he cried cheerfully. 'Did anyone ever ask Blake, "How do you get on with your mum and dad these days, Bill?"'

A short while after this conversation, he invited me to a party at his house, which was suitably large and full of character. His parents were out, or had been sent to wait in the woods somewhere. Though it sounds suspiciously like false memory syndrome, we did actually toboggan down the stairs on tea trays and throw sandwiches at each other. Cider raised a hectic flush on many a cheek; Tydeman honoured me with an illicit tumblerful of his father's amontillado. The music was provided by Sibelius, not an unpopular choice: there were enough juvenile string players present to fill most desks of the Hallé. Someone tall and willowy kissed me in the kitchen; a girl was sick out of the window and lost her specs to the dark.

Tydeman orchestrated this mayhem wearing a white shirt with a Byronic stock, his amply filled trousers cinched with a cummerbund.

'He has lapsed into French,' a solemn young man said, as our host recited Lamartine, one of the set books. 'Nothing but ill can come of this.'

'Who is that bloke over there?'

'Now why do you want to know that?'

'He kissed me in the kitchen.'

'He is a trainee quantity surveyor,' the solemn young man explained.

'"That is all ye know on earth, and all ye need to know,"' I quoted, convulsing a girl from Ware Girls' Grammar. She and I went out into the dark to look for the missing specs.

'Do you go to lots of these things?' she asked as we combed a shrub with our fingers.

'This is the first party I have ever been to.'

'Oh God, I've found the sick. Do you have a hanky? You're not going to tell me you're just a poor gypsy boy who wipes his nose on nettles?'

'You can sod off,' I said, huffed.

We were called back inside for a game called Murder in the Dark, about which I knew nothing and cared less. The girl from Ware sat next to me on Mrs Tydeman's chintzy sofa. She took my glass of Mr Tydeman's sherry from me and swigged. I was studying the pattern on the Turkish carpet and, as my mother would have put it, sulking my hat off. Everyone was trying to explain the rules of the game. Pieces of paper were passed around. Mine was blank. After much giggling, the lights went out.

The girl from Ware reached out in the dark and brushed her fingers against my cheek. This was so unexpected that for a moment I froze but then I pushed her back against the cushions and shoved my hand up her jumper. It met the resistance of a pretty substantial brassiere, anchoring impressively warm and bouncy breasts. Her hands circled my throat.

'This is nice,' she whispered, 'but I'm afraid I'm going to have to kill you.'

My more usual Saturday-night pleasures were taken with a loose gang of tearaways whose stamping ground was the Royal Ballroom at Tottenham, later immortalised in a sketch by Peter Cook and Dudley Moore. We went there to see and be seen, with the additional thrill of chancing – and it would have been an unlucky one – on the awesomely named Half-Brick Gang.

'Presumably because they eat half-bricks for breakfast.'

'That ain't funny,' said Terry, who lived near me. 'Those boys are the real thing. I mean they are bastards. You don't wanna mess with them. Oh dear, no.'

The top geezers in our mob went to the Royal by motor but Terry and I travelled to the meet by train. Coming home from a night of drinking Mann's bottled stout, we would select a compartment where respectable citizens and their wives were sitting with London theatre programmes on their knees.

'Go on, then, bung us a fag,' Terry would demand. He was little and dangerous and could be recognised as the genuine article by his peg-bottom trousers and a baby-blue jacket the length of a mac. When proffered a cigarette he would take the packet and stuff it in the patch pocket of his shirt.

'I just killed a bloke,' he explained one night to a terrorised couple.

'Why was that?'

'The geezer gives me a funny look. Same as you just done.'

Sometimes he would introduce me.

'He's done a few people an' all. Last week a big fat bloke called him a poof. So he shivved him and then cut his nose off. Still at school, but it's in the blood. Tell 'em where you come from.'

'Lambeth.'

'See?'

But then, more often than not, when we got back to the estate, Terry's dad would be waiting at the window of his house. At the first sight of us staggering up the road, he would come out and cuff his son.

'What kind of time d'you call this, you toerag? And you' – pointing at me – 'you can sling your hook, you skinny little bastard.'

'He doesn't like you because you're still at school,' Terry

explained. 'But then again, he doesn't like anyone down the Eastfields.'

Terry's house was located in Northfield Road, all of 150 yards away.

It was the occasional habit of the gang to rove nearer to home, arriving mob-handed at the door of local dances and chatting up the local talent. In November, I was tipped the wink that we would assemble for just such a rumble at a church hall on the Enfield highway the following Saturday. Either I got the instructions wrong or the gods of chance spared this place, for when I turned up there were no more than forty people present. I was wearing my father's overcoat and the brown zoot suit that had bowled Figgie over in her day, set off by yellow socks and a gold knitted tie. On my feet were the infamous brothel-creepers.

It says much for the good-natured neighbourhood that not one person batted an eyelid. The waltz was taken up by what seemed to me elderly couples. There was one exception. Two girls danced together, for want of a partner their own age. I walked the slim one home. She lived just around the corner in a little road of neat and comely villas. Like me, she was still at school.

Chapter Two

ONE OF MY FATHER'S FIRST ACTS OF IMPROVEMENT to his new property was to re-lay the lawn, watched covertly by Alf next door, who had young children and a huge romping sheepdog. For the Arnhem veteran and car mechanic, a lawn was somewhere for the kids to play and the dog to dig. Once a week his cheerful and buxom wife would go out and hoist the washing on the line, her passion killers next to his frayed underpants, the family sheets flapping beside them in a wind that came, as Bert explained, direct from the Urals. On wash days the dog did indeed leap and snap in a sort of Russian ecstasy, on one occasion pulling Mrs Alf's capacious bra from its pegs and savaging it like a day-old lamb.

We too had a washing line but it was not allowed to cross the sacred rectangle that my father was preparing for seed. Our lawn was laid on crushed clinker and built up from riddled soil skimmed from the rest of the garden, mixed with a sack or two of sharp sand. When finished it became a tourist attraction, in the sense that neighbours walking past along the cinder track at the rear of the properties would pause and stare.

The gardens were divided only by double-strand wire fences, so that it was possible (as I discovered the following summer) to see girls sunbathing ten or more houses away, or listen to family disputes shouted from the kitchen to the curly kale and rhubarb, bellowed by people never to be met with in the street. Some neighbours had wonky birdbaths in cast concrete decorating their back garden, others mysterious stores covered by tarpaulins weighed down by bricks and car tyres. Our lawn was our particular signature. At number 73, we believed in greensward, level to within a few thousandths of an inch.

The new neighbours were loud and matey because they saw themselves as being all in the same boat: short of the readies, up to their necks on the never-never, yet hoping for something better to come along when – particularly – Tony or Phil, Angie or June left school and started bringing in the dosh. Parliamentary politics, the future of Europe or any of the rest of the things that were supposed to engage them as voters and citizens were of no interest. So far as the world of ideas was concerned, they were out of the loop and they liked it that way.

'See that bloke there?' a man asked me in a reverent whisper while we were queuing for a bus. 'You'll never see a better darts player in your life.'

He was indicating the neighbour who lived exactly opposite us, whose name we did not know and who passed us in the street without an attempt at a greeting. I had marked him out as a citizen with grave concerns, silent because plunged in thought, his mind chewing on Life itself. It was a shock – but not an unpleasant one – to realise that he was more likely pondering the fabled nine-dart finish.

There were not yet cars in the street to polish or tinker with but it was the very beginning of home improvement. On most Sundays there was the yelp and rasp of saws as men fashioned occasional furniture from marine plywood and lengths of woolly battening. We never saw the finished results because in all the time we lived there we never entered another house. The Great Lawn of Waltham Cross was my father's contribution to the upward mobility of the neighbourhood. When he began to build a glazed lean-to, from whence my mother might sit and contemplate (but not walk upon) the lawn's awesome emeraldness, we had, so to speak, arrived.

Some of the materials for the lean-to came from a builder's yard on the Middlesex side of the county boundary and it was here that the father of the mystery girl from the dance worked. His name was George, a short, barrel-chested man with prematurely grey hair and a shy smile. To know George, you needed to know only one story. During the liberation of Rouen he had climbed across the rubble in an outlying village and presented a quarter-pound packet of army tea to a shell-shocked family sitting in the ruins of their house. He saw them as people like himself, though French, who could do with a decent brew-up to gather their wits. Whatever he said to them (and it would have been expressed in mime show) they kept the tea as undrinkable testimony to Allied good intentions. When I saw it in 1956, the packet stood unopened on its own little shelf in the rebuilt kitchen.

S, the girl from the dance, was an only child. Her dark hair was cut short, framing a snub-nosed face that was animated enough: when she laughed she doubled over, only coming upright again to wipe the tears from her eyes. But what made her laugh in the first place was absurdity and inappropriateness; her default expression was a chin-up and faintly challenging briskness. An amateur portrait photographer had tried to capture the essence of her and failed completely. In these pictures, she looked merely awkward and defensive. These were not portraits but interrogations of the observer.

Invited to tea one Sunday, I found the family had a piano that no one could play and a flatulent old dog called Mick. The house was solidly built but little. Downstairs there was nothing but a single room and a kitchen. The front door opened directly onto the stairs. George had a wooden garage at the end of the garden stored with half-empty paint tins, and had recently moved up from a motor-cycle and sidecar to a pale green Hillman, as lovingly tended as any racehorse. They ate proper breakfasts, this family, had weekend lunch with real cuts of meat, and on Sunday afternoons splashed out with a bit of cake and a tin of peaches, soused in Carnation milk.

'If it's so bloody wonderful round her house, go and live there,' my mother encouraged me, riddling the boiler that provided hot water. 'See if I give a bugger.'

It was tempting. Vi was as tall as George was short. An essential shyness made her talk too much, a garrulity he good-naturedly abridged. Yes, her family had been Cheshunt notables in their day – 'My father had two ladders,' she once confided – and yes, it was true that Uncle Alan was a parks superintendent for a big borough with many workers under his command. But as George pointed out, the fantasy that she knew the better parts of England like the back of her hand – castles, stately homes and little villages that time had forgot – came from holiday tourism and not first-hand acquaintance with the owners and occupants of these places.

'Have you never been to Devon?' she exclaimed. 'Oh, but it's lovely down there. Jamaica Inn and all that.'

'Now is Jamaica Inn really in Devon, dear?' he asked, casting me a sly glance.

'I know where I think it is,' Vi insisted, blushing.

On the other hand, they did talk to each other. S was a wonder to them: dutiful, horribly bright and more socially confident than both of them put together. One of the earliest memories I have of her is totalling her father's timesheets while he sat mute and disgraced, unable to say exactly how many hours he had put in when driving the firm's van and doing little painting and decorating jobs around about the neighbourhood. It was all of a piece with his army career: he worked, never complained, and if he said he'd show up, he'd be there. The money side of things was an uncomfortable mystery.

There was an earlier framed photograph of S looking winsome in gingham and sporting schoolgirl plaits, the perfect third-former. Like me, she was destined for ten O-levels and, like my parents, hers were having the greatest difficulty in understanding what that signified. The school – one of the best girls' grammar schools in the country – had already marked her out for a career in law or medicine. But what sounded so obvious in the teacher's common room arrived back home in a very different state.

It was Vi's opinion that for her daughter to go to university was out of the question – that would be for the family to overreach. After all, they had got by so far without once coming to the attention of the authorities. Maybe it seemed to Vi that only doctors' daughters or the children of gentry went to Oxford or Cambridge, where they doubtless swanned about in punts, drinking champagne out of silver mugs. I do not think it too fanciful to suggest that one of her antipathies to the idea of a university education was what to say to these toffs, were they ever to pitch up one Sunday afternoon for tinned peaches, dressed in tennis flannels fastened at the waist with the old school tie, yahooing and blowing hunting horns.

In that fatally damaging phrase, they knew their place, these two quiet people. It must have seemed very extraordinary to them that of all the young men she might have met, S had brought home such a badly drawn sketch of a university place-seeker, half yob, half swot, a boy who rolled his own cigarettes and was rendered speechless by the novelty of Battenberg cake. It never once entered their minds that their child was just as intelligent, rather better educated and twice as sane.

S and I had what we thought of as our first real date on my eighteenth birthday. It included a visit to Lyons Corner House in the Tottenham Court Road and looking back on it, both the word 'date'and the venue have a museum dustiness. It happened to be the Rugby League Challenge Cup Final that afternoon. To the novelty of the mechanised self-service belt, on which the customer placed his plate and then chased after it, flinging on his food, was added the presence of a few of the 89,000 fans who had recently decamped from what was still called the Wembley Empire Stadium. As northerners were as foreign to me as Tuaregs, we sat down with some pleasure at a table already taken by a very large man wearing a Huddersfield rosette the size of a cauliflower. He had much to celebrate in his quiet way, for the game had gone to Huddersfield, the winning try being scored by the nineteen-year-old Peter Ramsden.

This man, a family man, was eating a salad scrambled together from the absurd moving belt and he was no doubt reflecting on the shoddy peripherals that actually made up Wembley Glory. The lads had won, St Helens had been booed off the pitch, and now here he was eating what he didn't want in the company of a load of nesh Londoners. S noticed that he was shaking sugar onto his sliced tomatoes.

'Excuse me,' she said in a kindly way, 'that is not salt you've got hold of there.'

The fan from Huddersfield paused for a moment, the sugar shaker in his meaty fist. He sucked his teeth in a ruminative way, his pale eyes studying us as if we were all of a piece with metropolitan degeneracy.

'I like sugar on my tomatoes,' he said at last, spreading the last three syllables with rumbling emphasis.

He came from a different country than ours. Had he asked me to place Huddersfield on a map I could have done it by exploration with my finger-end but as to what it was like there and how he lived we had no idea. We were too terrified to ask him either. He chomped away in silence, casting us the occasional glance and rereading the match programme.

How shy we were. I was recognisable at a thousand paces as some sort of twitty schoolboy but S could be described with approval as a young woman, not – or not only – for her character but by the clothes she wore. We could have left Joe Lyons' that day and walked the length of Oxford Street without seeing a single garment marketed specifically for people our age. The generations had no gap and though the bough was creaking ominously, it had yet to break. There were no teenagers. The streets were peopled with trainee adults.

*

George and Vi were Winnie-lovers, devoted to the wartime leader for his stubborn defiance of the dictator whom Vi described as 'that old Hitler', but also seduced by what they saw as the cranky and even louche sides to Churchill's personality. The siren-suit, the brandy and cigars, the habit of dictating letters from the bath and holding court in bed, the passion for sea-bathing – all these were signs of a real gent. Churchill was their idea of a prime minister: doubtless a *Daily Express* reader like themselves but scaled up to titanic proportions. It was scandalous that he had been dumped out of office in 1945 and his return in October of 1951 was a triumph for common sense. His conduct towards the new Queen was judged to be impeccable.

I was having much more trouble reading the world. In our house, the only political commentary on offer was my father's, whose opinion it was that until we bombed Moscow to rubble in a sudden pre-emptive nuclear strike, no good could come of anything. (He himself was perfectly willing to come out of retirement to sit at the navigator's desk on such a worthwhile and historic sortie.) All I had to oppose this lunacy was a sort of little-magazine radicalism. Somewhere, perhaps in Paris, perhaps in Greenwich Village, was a garret where truth was being trumpeted. Fat chance it had of being heard but that did not diminish the sweetness of its tone. It was, I imagined, the kind of exhilarated testimony that went along with Charlie Parker recordings, cheap wine and sex with Scandinavians.

The materials for this fantasy were to hand. Andrew Wilkinson arranged for us to use the reserve stacks of the County Library, just across the road from school. His intention was for us to read, for example, the whole of Wordsworth's *Prelude* and not just the abridged school text. And so some boys did just that. But I found myself endlessly sidetracked by material not to be met with in the syllabus. The first words I ever read about Picasso were those printed in Janet Flanner's collection of New Yorker pieces, *An American in Paris*. The detail I remember best is her carefully crafted throwaway remark about how, when he was young and poor, the artist painted pictures on the wall of all the furniture his garret did not possess. That struck me as being an admirable way to carry on.

Another blind alley was *Vidocq*, the autobiography of the founder of the French Sûreté. It came in an English translation of 1928 and, though racy enough to fill anyone's afternoon, there was little evidence that the original language in which it was written was French. Was it genuine, even, or a literary spoof? I consulted Andrew Wilkinson.

'Do you know,' he said wryly, 'it's a question I have never asked myself. On the other hand, I think about the *Prelude* all the time. I was going to ask you: would you like to come to tea on Sunday?'

This invitation, when relayed to my mother, created unromantic havoc.

'That's it! I knew it! Well, we'll soon set the police on *him*.

Where does he live? Don't tell me – he's got a lovely little cottage out in the country, far away from prying eyes. Eh?'

'He's married.'

'Ha!' my mother cried. 'But he still picked *you* out all right. And no wonder! Walking around with books of bloody poems under your arm! Mincing down the street with your la-di-da haircut and your yellow socks!'

'Who is this Wilkinson?' my father asked bluntly when he too was told about the invitation.

'He's a Ph.D.'

'That's not what I asked. Who is he?'

'Look, I have a load of catching up to do. Everybody at that school is brighter than me, with more background, more general knowledge, more everything.'

'So this is some sort of remedial class?'

'If you like, yes.'

The idea pleased him – not that Wilkinson was taking pains with my education but that I stood in need of such help. A few days earlier, Figgie had signalled the end to our undying devotion by returning a dress that I had won for her in a newspaper competition. It came cut up in postage-stamp-size coupons. There was nothing else in the parcel – no note, no tearstained farewell. It was like the roar of the lioness out on the veldt and I took it to mean that my supplanter, Ian, had failed to come up to scratch and had left her wounded but defiant. Or maybe they were sublimely happy and Figgie had chosen this way to make that apparent. Either way, Bert thought it the funniest thing to have happened for years. Chortling, he took a handful of the little squares from the dustbin and showed them over the fence to Alf next door.

Wilkinson did indeed live out in the country, down the lane from Henry Moore's workshops. I arrived for tea wearing my school blazer, bought from a shop in the Cross that catered for the sort of people who belonged to bowls clubs, and wearing a precautionary and sober tie. I was greeted at the door by the cheerfully haphazard Mrs Wilkinson. Her bare feet scrunched the scattered pages of the Sunday papers and she hoisted the waistband of her skirt in the way that sailors do when dancing the hornpipe, elbows akimbo. I was expected (for a moment I thought I had caught them in the bedroom) but no great preparation had been made for my arrival. Mrs Wilkinson's smile was warm and friendly.

'I'm making some tea soon. Andrew's in there,' she said, pointing to a side room.

He was even more casually dressed than his wife, his hair tousled, his chin unshaven, feet jammed into a pair of unlaced tennis shoes. The tiny room was almost entirely filled by a trestle table, on which were laid the page proofs to a schools edition of Blake. He smiled his own crooked smile of welcome.

'I feel guilty about this,' he said, waving his arm at the scene. 'I mean I don't think Jack or Jill ever envisioned this as a study when they lived here. Maybe the pig had it.'

'Have I stopped you working?'

'I was proof-reading,' he explained, not without a little flick of vanity. 'I also read your stuff in here and mark books from the lower school. There's no heating but that's good too. For optimum conditions in our kind of work you need warm feet and a cool head. Double socks are the answer.'

It swept over me in an instant, standing in that little space with cranky windows looking onto fields and hedges, that man and wife *could* be happy and that the life of the intellect was in many ways quite as prosaic as driving a bus or digging holes in the roadway. Andrew Wilkinson was susceptible to the same life-saving ordinariness – of teething babies and broken furniture, improvised weekends and grinding hard work – as our neighbour Alf.

'Is your wife a graduate?' I asked.

'I'm afraid so. We, um, pretend to the neighbours that we're itinerant farm labourers, of course. Let me show you how to mark up a proof. See that little squiggle there? It reverses the order of the letters.'

The tea that had been promised was a knife and fork affair – ham and eggs and a baked potato. The potato had the same curiosity value as the cottage itself: was this genuinely what posh people ate at five on a Sunday?

We talked; or rather, they talked and I limped after. It was amazing to hear her contradict him with such vehemence, only to burst out laughing a few moments later at some sly riposte. He was very pleased with her and I knew enough about men to see that he was showing her off. Gradually, I grasped much more clearly what was happening: they were in love and unconsciously they wanted me to share in that, to notice and approve it. There could hardly have been a greater compliment to a gauche boy, such as I was.

'What do you know about Vidocq?' Andrew asked her when we were at table.

'Nothing. Is it a Metro station?'

He indicated with a forkful of baked potato that I should expound.

'He's a Frenchman. He's not important. Or maybe he's very important. I wouldn't know which.'

'That's the ticket,' she said.

'I am trying to get this boy to concentrate all his talents and make them flow in a single direction,' he complained.

'Why do you let him call you a boy?' she asked, quite accidentally thrilling me to the marrow. Andrew laughed.

'This candidate, then. This student. This young man.'

Mrs Wilkinson smiled.

'He is shy of calling you by your first name, for fear that you should think him patronising. Do you have a girl?'

'Yes.'

'Then tell us all about her. Tell me. How long have you known her? Do you go to London together?'

'You may prefer to write your answers, using one side of the paper only,' her husband murmured.

'Does she read?' Mrs Wilkinson asked.

'Novels. About people like you,' I said, entranced.

The glances they exchanged were swift and private.

The village was served by a single-decker bus that ran every hour and a half. When the time came to say goodbye, I was posted out of the door to meet it under some dripping trees, changed my mind and set off walking. The rain drifted across sodden fields and the road was empty. For once in my life I had seen an opportunity at the very moment that it was presented to me and not months or years after, when it was all too late. It came in the form of a proposition. I too could live like a Wilkinson.

A possible stumbling block was an almost complete ignorance of the human ordinariness I so much admired. S's father George knew more about the dynastic history of England than I ever would. But he also knew about putty and sandpaper, tiles and guttering, four-stroke combustion engines and the vagaries of the carburettor. He knew the varieties of tits and finches that plundered his garden but also the principal bottlenecks to be encountered along the North Circular. All this was information he liked to share.

An orphan child, he had found his true family in the Scout movement, of which he was now a senior and indispensable member, a sort of unromantic good egg, the bloke who gets the rations through, no matter what the weather. In the most unobtrusive way, he belonged. I was used to cocky and highly combative Londoners. He was a fully fledged

Englishman: slow, unjudging, curious about the little things and, in his own way, learned.

'Why,' he said at once when told of the location of Andrew Wilkinson's cottage, 'that's where Mr Moore does his sculpture.'

My Uncle Jim knew about Henry Moore but my father did not. He associated all art with suede shoes and Balkan Sobranies. Art was not a process but an illness.

There was at school a Hale Society, for which one stood for election by presenting a paper on some scholarly subject. I scraped in by outlining the contribution made to human understanding by Duke Ellington, though stymied at the last moment by a point of order from the floor, asking whether it was permissible to illustrate the question by recordings. A vote was taken and the point of order upheld. My talk on Ellington thus became a checklist of names and dates, painful to deliver and excruciating to hear. I would have done better and suffered fewer interruptions by speaking on, say, the forest-floor flora of the Burmese uplands. But the substance of the talk was hardly to the point. This was an essay in manners. Anyone peering through the window would have witnessed half a dozen know-alls in school blazers playing at being eighteenth-century gentlemen.

'Point of information, Chair. Can the speaker further elucidate the derivation of the noun phrase "East St Louis Toodle-oo"?'

'In what regard?'

'I was wondering whether any other living American has used the word "toodle-oo" in common speech.'

'Your point is vexatious and I cannot allow it.'

'Point of order, Mr Chair, a point of information can surely not of itself be held to be vexatious?'

'Oh, do shut up.'

The following day, a few of us rambled upstream along one of the four rivers that run into Hertford, talking similar nonsense, denigrating our betters and making reckless pledges about the future. Our audience was ducks and the occasional water rat. It came to me that what we were after was something much more troublesome than showing off a little learning to the otherwise peaceful landscape. The formalities of the Hale Society, the insufferable pomposity deemed appropriate when speaking to the County Library staff, the cheery contempt showered on the estimable Dr Bunt: all of this was a not very well coded desire to acquire the language of the Establishment.

For some it was a matter of inheritance. Tydeman, for example, lived in what was for me a big house and had rich parents. Going up to Cambridge (which he was to do with great success) was just a further step along the road. Another boy had obtained permission from the headmistress of Ware Girls' Grammar to take cranial measurements of the sixth form with a pair of home-made calipers. His credentials were bespoke: both parents were doctors. It was only when he was discovered using his calipers to measure the distance in centimetres between the nipples of a few of his more willing subjects that he was shown the door.

It was an affectation among some of the sixth form, heartily encouraged by Dr Bunt, who sent along the school copy (after having completed the crossword), to read *The Times*'s first leader as a daily intellectual exercise. Only a little background would have made this more palatable. The congerie of (largely) Oxford graduates assembled in Printing House Square were hardly addressing as their first audience a bunch of swotty youths having trouble with French irregular verbs or the niceties of Pope's poetic diction. Indeed, it was sometimes difficult to see to whom they addressed their thoughts at all, unless to another Fellow of All Souls, either hidden in the Government, or perhaps eating his toast and marmalade on the sovereign soil of a British Embassy. Bunt could not help us here: for him *The Times* was a national institution in the same way as were the Church of England, the Household Cavalry or the Marylebone Cricket Club.

'These Russians,' he asked me once, when making a pastoral visit to an otherwise deserted classroom, 'can they truly keep knocking bricks out of the wall without the whole bang shoot coming down around their ears?'

'I don't think I understand, sir.'

'Aren't some things timeless? Must we challenge *every-thing*?'

He wandered away, a good man sensing the ground

tremble under his feet. It was the year that *The Mousetrap* opened in London and the Americans exploded the first hydrogen bomb on Eniwetok Atoll. Gentlemen of Bunt's kind, whose attachment to the Establishment was that of a limpet to its rock, were facing extinction.

As *The Times* reported in October, a state of emergency was declared in Kenya in order to fight the Mau Mau insurgency. Though I did not know it then, hundreds of bewildered Bunts were summoned from their farms and offices and mustered in Nairobi for service in the Kenya Regiment. It is said that when the roll was called, several retired brigadiers and a hatful of half-colonels were shown to be present on parade. They expected to be deployed in the city to combat riots and to break up unlawful assemblies; it was startling and, for old hands, a matter of great foreboding to find that the terrorists had fled to the forests. I read this news item with only passing interest and forgot it almost as soon as I turned the page.

The least part of my knowledge concerning the Establishment was to do with royalty. It was often mentioned in conversations about the Blitz that when the King and Queen visited the East End, Elizabeth wore her best clothes and finest hats, on the basis that she was being invited to people's homes, even though those might be in smoking ruins. She was sure that, were the dazed people she met ever to visit the Palace, they would pay her the same compliment.

The new Queen was best remembered from those times as a plump young woman in a tailored ATS uniform, posing as the driver of a one-ton truck. Had she worn a crisp blue poplin shirt and tie and been photographed as a WAAF plotter, my father might have thought better of her. Hardly a republican, he nevertheless sensed, in the clumsy spin that created the idealised notion of a Royal Family, a cruel reproach to his own marital situation. My mother agreed.

'Give me a couple of hundred servants and four separate gaffs to live in and you'd see some flag-waving then.'

'Queen Ada,' my father scoffed.

'Me and His Royal Highness here,' she retorted, pointing to my brother. 'The international playboy.'

'And Spurs' inside-right,' Neil added.

Over at George and Vi's, the royals were seen in a very different light. However deferentially, we were talking about old friends or, better still, watching a much-loved film, weak on plot but stuffed with colourful characters, often shown to their best advantage at funerals. The late King had never wanted the job in the first place. Though he wore the uniforms well and disguised his lifelong illnesses with great dignity, he had been at his happiest as the Duke of York, sitting in a circle at a Scout jamboree, singing and miming to the song 'Underneath the Spreading Chestnut Tree'. His much more sparky wife could never forgive her brother-in-law David for running off with a divorcée when he had the Empire to look after. The two princesses were both beautiful, but whereas one was flighty and a bit fun-loving – naughty even – the other was the very model of duty.

The Coronation of Elizabeth II was set for 2 June. Though the event was to be televised, S considered it essential to be present in London on that day. After a few demurrals, I went with her the night before to the corner of Northumberland Avenue and Whitehall, or, putting it in more gracious Royal-speak, opposite Admiralty Arch. And a damp dawn we had of it. Far away in Tibet, the conquerors of Mount Everest had been persuaded to delay the news of their ascent to coincide with the day of the investiture. It provided more drama than what little could be seen from our vantage point: a procession of coaches and the heads of marching columns. Though we had bought souvenir editions of the papers to keep and treasure, they had more use to us as mats on which to stand and in the end to sit, as damp as seaweed and with splitting headaches.

Three million citizens turned out in London and – or so it seemed – everyone else in the country was watching the events on television. The RAF flew tapes across the Atlantic by Canberra and jet fighter so that Her Majesty's loyal Canadian subjects could enjoy the show on the day of its happening. We were in the midst of hysteria. But the detail I like best about that wet day in London is that the Royal Household had nowhere near enough carriages and coachmen of its own to transport the honoured guests. The shortfall was made up by private persons, described in one report as 'millionaires and country squires', who donated their vehicles and – necessarily – themselves as coachmen and footmen. For this loyal service, they were required to dress in livery. Thackeray could not have invented better.

As for S and me, we kissed and fondled as young people do, though never in the presence of grown-ups. On one occasion I renewed my acquaintance with allotment sheds when we went to shelter in George's on the way home from the cinema in pelting rain. Only two years earlier this would have been the prequel to unbridled sexual incendiarism (LOCAL MAN'S SHALLOTS IN MYSTERY BLAZE, WAR VETERAN BAFFLED). Though we cuddled, nothing followed from it. The rain lashed down, the spiders shrank into their corners, trains clattered past. The earth was huger and rounder than it had been when I lived in Cambridge: this was a girl who placed enormous value on where things led. We spent a good deal of time imagining tomorrow, for me a novel way of going on.

'Don't you ever think about having your own front door?'
'Erm—'
'Not round here. Far away from here.'

No one could mistake the animal trace of youthful sex, for it was the only semi-public expression of appetite in a society that liked to lock itself in at night. The back-seat stalls of cinemas, in summer the more remote parts of public parks, in winter bus shelters, were all cockpits of desire. A few doors down from us in the Eastfields was a girl renowned for keeping her knickers in her handbag. When she fell pregnant, her father and uncle found the father, a boy of nineteen, and spoke a few persuasive words to him about iron bars and broken legs. They were married a month later. Naturally, the bride wore white. She left for the church in a rented Rolls-Royce, chucking her cig into her dad's cotoneasters.

'Someone's put her up the stick,' my mother commented. 'You want to watch it. It only takes a second.'

'A second what?' Neil asked, intrigued.

'I don't suppose it's any good telling you that not everybody's sex barmy?' I demanded, blushing.

'No,' Peggy said. 'It's not.'

As soon as I had completed all the S-level papers, my father found me a temporary job as a furniture porter at Fishpools, a shop in the Cross that passed for a department store. My fellow porters were a rum lot, very economical in speech and habits. We drank tea and studied the horses, while the hugely fat foreman slept off the night before on piles of blankets. From time to time we would be sent out in the van to deliver rolls of carpet and lino, armchairs, beds and the like. What I had sensed about how people saw me in Eastfield Road was reinforced by these little excursions.

'He ain't much use, I shouldn't think,' a grim old woman said, pointing to me after Nobby and I had manhandled a new mattress up her stairs. She spoke as if I were deaf, or simple-minded.

'It's like dogs. Look at his feet. He ain't grown into his

full size yet. When he's put on a stone or two, there'll be no stopping him.'

'Why's his hair all long?'

This untaxing work was overseen by a clerk who had been in end-of-the-pier shows and, much earlier in his life, a chorus boy in West End revues. Jack still had the hips and the silvery barnet that went with his former profession, although, as he confided, his legs were ruined. He sat in a little cubbyhole all by himself, reading *The Stage* and from time to time emitting howls of disbelieving laughter at the success of old chums.

'Ethne Summersley! Unbelievable!'

'You and him have a lot in common,' Nobby advised me. 'You was both took by the fairies when you was kids.'

My father pocketed the money got from this job, giving me back the loose change. For once, there was nothing vindictive about his reasons; by his own lights he was teaching me how to contribute to the family income. There were only two ways of doing this. You could either tip up – that is, donate your entire pay packet by emptying it on the draining board of the kitchen sink – or pay board. The wage for being a trainee furniture porter was so negligible that tipping up was the only choice.

One night Bert came home and found me reading the examination results for English and French at S-level. I had distinctions in both subjects. The stage was set for one of his most memorable utterances. He gave the paper back to me and lit a cigarette. His eyes were dangerous.

'So what happens now?'

'I stay on for the seventh term and go for a open scholarship to university.'

My mother was watching us, a saucepan of mashed potatoes in her hand. Neil was drawing moustaches on that night's pictures in the *Evening Standard*.

'You listen to me,' Bert said, with the authority of a bishop. 'You've read enough bloody books in your lifetime.'

When I laughed incredulously, he waved the sound away, as if brushing cobwebs.

'You *don't* go back to school, you get in the army and let them make a man of you.'

'I've told them I'd go back if I got the right grades.'

'Well,' he said. 'Untell them. You've had your notice from the National Service. That comes first. You can't welch on the Government, you'll find *that* out soon enough.'

'I could get an exemption.'

'Oh yes, very bloody likely.'

'Listen to what Hitler says,' my mother put in. But her eyelids pricked with tears.

To sign on for the soldiers, as Peggy put it, meant a visit to Wanstead, to the sort of building that had walls that wept and windows that had not been cleaned since Monty brought the Wehrmacht to justice at Lüneberg Heath. Anybody who has served his National Service will remember the faintly salty smell of damp concrete and stale cigarettes that places like this exude.

I was interviewed by an elderly captain in uniform, sitting behind a War Department desk with a telephone and some empty wire filing baskets for company. It happened to be a warm day outside and there was a pantomime moment when this gatekeeper to the armed forces tried to open a window. I was too awed to offer to help him. He banged fretfully for a while on the rusting iron frame with the butt end of a ruler before giving up and sitting down.

He began the interview by lying through his teeth.

'My job is to place you in the branch of the service best suited to your background and aptitudes.'

'I was hoping to join the Navy.'

'That's what they all say. Nor, to head you off, does the RAF want any more fighter pilots. Do you have a second language?'

'French.'

'Useless. You don't speak Russian?'

'No.'

He waited patiently for me to grasp the nettle.

'I wouldn't mind joining the Tank Corps,' I said after an excruciating silence.

'Interesting. And why would you want to do that?'

'I would like to learn how to drive.'

At once his face darkened and he leaned forward across the desk.

'Now don't try to get funny with me, sonny. You're not signing up for some holiday camp. This isn't Butlin's.'

'Well, the paratroopers then,' I suggested, thinking of Alf and his laconic account of sitting in a three-storey Dutch house in Nijmegen so riddled with holes that some German shells passed clean through it, from front to back. According to Alf, they made a riffling noise, like thumbing briskly through the telephone book.

The captain studied me, made a few notes on a loose sheet of paper and silently indicated the door. When I was out in the street – a moody and indifferent Civvy Street strewn with cabbage leaves from some morning market – I could see him attacking the jammed window to his office with the heel of his shoe.

Chapter Three

TODAY IT IS USUAL – ESPECIALLY AMONG THOSE who have never faced conscription – to describe National Service as time wasted, even an offence against civil liberties in some sinister way.

'One thing is certain,' bristling young ideologues have explained to me, as if to some balding warmonger with blood on his hands, 'you would never get our generation to take part. We have come a long way since then. We know far more.'

It is the last sentence that always stops me in my tracks. For me, National Service was a blizzard of people and ideas I never knew existed. The gates of a very small purgatory were about to open, casting light onto cheerful chaos, shot through with insanity and heroism in about equal measure.

I spent the first night burning the pimples out of ammunition boots with the back of a spoon heated over a candle; and writing to a girl called Alma, whose illiterate husband Tony had yesterday been cleaning vats at Mann's brewery.

'What do you want me to say?' I asked, holding his warm sixpence in the palm of my hand.

'It ain't difficult. Just that I'm here and all that.'

So saying, he set off with his mates for a cup of tea.

Kempston Barracks, Bedford, was the home of the Beds and Herts, whose regimental history had been given to us earlier in the day by the adjutant. To hear his remarks we had been herded like sheep into the chapel, which even to my untutored eye had an air of disuse about it. This being the army, there was due deference to the outward forms expected of a place of worship: the pews glistened and the brass lectern shone. While nobody much cared about the word of God in the ranks of the Beds and Herts, if He ever wanted to utter it in a local setting He would find the place buffed to a nicety.

It was a mild September afternoon and bars of sunlight fell in military precision. Some of the recruits slept, their newly shorn skulls dropping to their chests in emotional exhaustion. The adjutant concluded his historical sketch by dabbing at his lips with a crisply folded handkerchief. When he invited questions, a hand shot up.

'Yes?'

'When do we get our first leave, mate?'

There was a skittering of hobnails on the marble floor as a sergeant plucked this unfortunate questioner from his pew and frogmarched him outside. When we filed out ourselves a few moments later, he was doubling around the parade ground with an empty dustbin raised above his head.

'Everything's fine. I have already made some good mates. A lot of us are from north London but some are from the country areas. The barracks are not all that old but made to look that way, like a fort in an Alexander Korda movie.'

I considered this last touch, wondering how many Korda movies Alma had seen in her short life. She might be much more interested in Private Wood, who had not stopped crying since his arrival, or Private Tasker, a man-mountain for whom the stores could not supply a uniform big enough. Tasker sat opposite me while I wrote, scratching his shins absent-mindedly, undressed to his drawers/cellular/green, the one item of army clothing sized to fit all. What Tasker called his crown jewels dangled free, not – or not only – because they were in scale with the rest of him, but rather that the drawers themselves were such sorry sketches of male under-wear.

'Tell her how much he misses her,' he suggested. 'And chuck in his best regards to the mother-in-law.'

'She might be dead.'

'They never are,' Tasker muttered. 'Don't you have a girl of your own to write to?'

'Yes. How about you?'

'Promised someone a line from time to time. But what can you say about all this?'

He had a point, almost immediately sharpened by the approach of the lance corporal in charge of our barrack room.

'Put some clothes on,' he said to Tasker. 'This isn't a nancy-boy parlour.'

Lance Corporal Denison was lately a squaddie just like ourselves. He had his own little room and, earlier in the evening, had sauntered out to show us how to improve our trousers by applying wet soap to the interior of the crease before ironing. Explaining how to bone boots, he showed us his own, cradled in his arms as lovingly as twins. The problem with Denison was that he wore glasses, was quite short, and had almost certainly been the butt of the playground bully in a previous existence. Only a little power over others had gone to his head now. Tasker stood, towering over him, all ivory skin and ginger fuzz.

'Fuck off, sonny,' he said.

Denison was about to put him on a fizzer when someone ran in from the ablutions. Private Wood had stopped crying long enough to drink a tin of liquid Brasso. He was, this messenger explained, spewing his ring and looked a funny colour. Purple, in fact.

We were all eighteen but that was the only thing we had in common. The letter I had written to Alma was no more than the truth: we came from different backgrounds and had seen very different things. The days when the regiment had been raised from amiable giants like Tasker had long gone. Wood's sad story was that he was, in the language of the day, queer – and, it was whispered, in love with a married Scoutmaster from Southall. His experiments with Brasso had placed him at death's door. He was taken away by civilian ambulance, covered in a blanket.

In our lot, as we spoke of the unselected rabble who slept and ate together, there were people like myself who had just finished a sixth-form course and others who were strangers to the written word, including Ronnie the Burglar and Fat Mick, who owned and raced greyhounds under his father's name. In these underlit and ghost-haunted barracks I met my first public schoolboy, an earnest big-ears called Henry, and my first real psychopath, a highly troubled Londoner by the name of Puckworth.

We marched; we saluted; we learned never to speak until spoken to. The drill sergeant was an old sweat with a ruined nose and watery eyes. In the time-honoured traditions of his calling, he swore on his mother's grave that we were the worst recruits he had ever been lumbered with.

'Even the bleedin' Gyppos would send you home in disgrace, you horrible bunch of pox-doctors' clerks. Puckworth, I seen lamp-posts in the street with more feeling for left and right than what you have got.'

'Garn, piss off,' Puckworth 371 replied. Somehow or other his head had shrunk since being issued with its beret, so that he stood in the ranks like a circus clown, vexed and ill-tempered. Sergeant Morris raised his eyes to a weeping heaven. His arms swept up in urgent semaphore.

'Tell me I never heard that, O Lord. Tell me I am dreaming.'

Rendering scenes like this in chatty form, to be read by a newly appointed bank clerk rattling through north London on the way to work, was beyond me, as was the huffing and grunting after lights out as thirty or so squaddies masturbated gloomily, bedsprings twanging. Some did it in despair (I supposed) and some to exhibit an anarchical freedom over bodies that were otherwise the annexed property of Her Majesty the Queen. Some, because it was their nightly ritual; and some because the susurration and mingled groans were in themselves highly erotic.

'Ouf!' Puckworth yelped at the other end of the room. 'Take that!'

It was the genius of the army to have placed the public schoolboy Henry in the next bed.

'Your sister's a very lucky girl, Puckers,' he drawled in the dark, forcing a shout of laughter from the rest of us that brought Lance Corporal Denison racing out from his cubby-hole.

On the fourth day, we were summoned one by one to take a Basic Aptitude Test, held in a small office and invigilated over by a dusty-looking captain with an air of such general unhappiness as to wring the heart. He laid out the tools of his trade on a green baize cloth.

'Now, in this box I have an object that I want you to take to pieces down to its last component and then reassemble. I shall time you with this stopwatch. You will begin on my word of command. Have you understood the instructions?'

'Yessir,' I said, not without dread. I was imagining some arcane piece of military equipment, or possibly something familiar but dangerous, like a loaded revolver. The captain fiddled about, experimenting with the stopwatch buttons. Tension mounted.

'Go!' he shouted suddenly.

Inside the box was a bicycle lamp.

'That was quick,' the captain said when I had finished. He searched his papers for an explanation. 'Ah, yes. I note that you have only just left school.'

'Yessir. But my grandparents had a bicycle repair shop and that helped.'

'And you? Do you think you could lead men? Are you a natural leader?'

'I shouldn't think so.'

This disappointed him. He stared at the time it had taken me to play with the bicycle lamp, a result he had scribbled down on a scrap of feint-ruled paper.

'Let me give you a piece of advice. Next time someone asks you a question about leadership, say you think of little else. Otherwise you'll be pushing swill buckets about for two years of your life. I suppose you're going to university?'

'I haven't applied anywhere.'

We sat in silence for a few moments, the captain plucking gloomily at his nose with a thumb and forefinger. Both of us were thinking about college scarves and muffins toasted on gas fires, guileless girls with their legs tucked up under them on chunky chintz sofas. Behind them the door to the bedroom was open.

In the end, six of the intake were issued with rail warrants and told to attend Officer Pre-Selection in Bury St Edmunds. As a subtle punishment for being educated beyond the true needs of the army, we were also ordered to take with us on the journey a huge mound of boots, tied together by their laces and with their owners' identities written on cardboard tickets. When we asked for a truck to the station, it raised a hollow laugh.

'There's six on you,' the guard commander pointed out. 'And you can always get a few grannies to help if the going gets tough. Now don't you go losing them boots. They'm on their way to Korea, once some real soldiers have got their feet in them.'

The epic passage of these boots from Bedford to Bury St Edmunds was eased on the first part of the journey because the train to Cambridge had a guard's van, where we sat tying the loose ones back onto the heap, our heads hanging low in shame. Nobody with such a fretful parcel, about the size of two armchairs, should also have had the ignominy of having to ask directions to the station. It was that period of our island history when it was thought richly comic to shout at squaddies, 'Thank God we've got a Navy,' a taunt we heard several times. Helpful old biddies stopped to point as we ran back for the stray boots, soon numbered in dozens. Four of us to drag the main pile, two to follow after with armfuls of unmatched footwear. The pavement behind us was littered with little squares of cardboard.

At Cambridge, though things had gone badly, we felt half our troubles were over. We ate the huge and fluffy cheese sandwiches provided by the cookhouse and drank mugs of tea from the station buffet. Henry, the public schoolboy, was our unofficial leader, not because he was especially resourceful but rather that he was the first to propose that, whatever happened, we could not be blamed for doing our best. He repeated this so often that it finally became clear to everyone that blame was heading our way like a gale of frogs. We lay against the boots, smoking and worrying.

When the connection to Bury St Edmunds arrived, we found to our horror that it had no guard's van and, much worse, it was a corridor train. A surprising number of people were already seated as we turned the pyramid of boots into a ramshackle leather wall, waist high, which we fed into the corridor with only seconds to spare before the train moved off. At every stop, we had to shuffle the boots this way and that to allow passengers to alight. The ticket guard was incensed. Henry explained.

'These boots are going to men who will soon be fighting for your freedom. Accordingly, they must get through.'

'I never seen nothing like it in all my life,' the guard bellowed.

'Neither have I,' Henry admitted. 'But there you are.'

It was dusk when we reached Bury St Edmunds and a

sharp rain was falling. A kindly porter, who identified himself as a former REME lance-jack, suggested ringing Gibraltar Barracks and demanding – not requesting, *demanding* – transport. Henry followed him into a hut on the station and was gone some while. When he came out, he looked ashen under the sputtering gas lamps.

'It isn't far, apparently, and quite easy to find.'

We began rolling the boots like a snowball down the glistening wet pavements, jeered by incredulous crowds on their way to a boxing match in the town centre. Our morale was low, to the point where we kicked along the boots that had broken free, like sulky schoolboys. We reached the barracks drenched to the skin. A slitty-eyed Corporal of the Guard emerged from the gatehouse.

'It's a joke, ennit? Some kind of bleedin' joke. Straighten yourselfs up. Tie them loose boots back on. Put your berets on straight and tuck them trousers back into them gaiters—'

He stopped to snap a salute at the Officer of the Day ambling around the corner, a young subaltern with an unfriendly moustache.

'Who are these horrible soldiers, Cor' Tanner?'

'Well, sir—'

'Horrible or not, we've brought your bloody boots from Bedford,' Henry interrupted, matching the lieutenant drawl for drawl.

He was immediately charged with insubordination and failing to address an officer in the correct manner. The rain lashed down on us all and there was a great deal of shouting and carrying on. We at least had been expected, but the boots not. Things were worse than that, even. These boots, in all their disarray, had technically ceased to exist – we had accidentally left the manifest or movement order or whatever (a smudged sheet of woolly paper) on the train. Though they were staring us in the face and filling with rain, on paper they had no being.

Gibraltar Barracks was the depot of the Suffolk Regiment. The barrack houses were nineteenth century and the ablution blocks – the wooden 'spiders' where those who needed to shave in the morning could do so in icy-cold water – dated from the recent war, though in the officers' mess there was silver going back to a much earlier age. The Suffolks were a proud bunch and liked a bit of swank with their soldiering. The drill sergeant, an impressive figure who would have done well at Rorke's Drift, was the superbly named Sergeant Holyoake. Mustered on the foggy parade ground, we would hear him long before we could see him, his heels cracking out a tattoo on the sanded tarmac. Holyoake had a genuine gift for humour.

'I had tinned tomatoes with my sausage this morning. That is horrible food. That is runny and – here is *my* word for it – disappointing. That don't look like no effing tomato I ever seen. No matter, says I to Sergeant Cleaver. I will curb my disappointment. I have my boys to look forward to.'

His voice rose to a roar.

'Only to come on here and see men – grown men – make them tinned tomatoes look like effing works of art. Make them look like effing horticultural *gods*.'

We potential officers were grouped together in one squad of thirty men, drawn from three regiments. Unfortunately for all of us, we had a real madman in our midst. He began modestly by scraping the design from the lid of his tin of Cherry Blossom and polishing the raw metal. Soon enough, we all had to do it. Then he found that the iron frame of his bed would receive boot blacking and we were all forced to do this too. The floor drew his attention next and we bleached the pine boards white with soap powder. This left the nail heads looking shabby until this man – who was destined to be an officer and so in theory lead men into battle against heartless Russians – hit on the expedient of polishing them with Brasso. We were so much in the grip of hysteria that, on the occasion of one inspection, we cleaned the room, made up our beds (walking about in socks the while) and agreed to sleep in the lavatory.

There was one problem: Henry, gangling, muddled and – as far as bullshit was concerned – ineducable. The madman hit on an idea, and if it seems absurd now, at the time it made good sense. Henry's bed, locker, equipment and everything else was posted through a hatch in the ceiling and the remaining beds artfully arranged to conceal the gap. After breakfast, still in his pyjamas, he was likewise boosted into the roofspace. Like the boots from Bedford, he had temporarily ceased to exist.

And we would have got away with it, until the moment when, alone in the dark, Henry missed his footing and plunged one pyjamaed leg through the barracks ceiling, showering the Adjutant and Sergeant Holyoake with plaster. The ghost of Hamlet's father never made a more dramatic appearance, nor uttered such a feeble entrance line.

'Sorry about that,' he called out indistinctly. 'Bloody miserable up here.'

The madman's hash was settled by an inter-platoon boxing tournament, in which the potential officer cadets were matched with the regular Suffolk intake, weight for weight, irrespective of experience. At the time I weighed ten stone four pounds and the only boxing I had done was being banged about in the back garden by my father. I searched out my opponent, whose ten stone four was distributed very differently. He was a farm boy barely five feet six tall. Bribery was useless: he was going to kill me.

'Rubbish,' the madman in our ranks snapped. 'Boxing's a science.'

I fought the bout immediately after his, getting into a ring slippery with blood and snot. He himself was in an ambulance, on the way to hospital with a fractured jaw.

The place where I had tried to bribe my opponent was the NAAFI hut, in which pleasure was measured out in pennies:

tea, a butterless scone, on pay day ten Woodies or a half-ounce block of Golden Virginia. One night, I sat down with a bit of their headed notepaper and wrote to Trinity College, Cambridge, brushing crumbs of Bakewell tart from the text. Of Trinity, I knew only that it was a big college. My story was brief. Trinity had never heard of me but I had things to offer that might interest them: desire, ambition, devotion to scholarship, a full heart. I sealed the envelope without knowing that very few students of English were admitted there.

I received a laconic reply, saying that never before had the author received a letter from the NAAFI, that the grades I had mentioned were most impressive (my first experience of time-less academic sarcasm) and that he greatly regretted that my present situation made an interview (or so he must suppose) difficult to arrange. I read so far with blushing embarrass-ment, only to choke on the last sentence. In light of the circumstances, therefore, he would waive normal procedures and was pleased to offer me a place in October 1955.

I showed this amazing letter to Henry, who suggested I write a carefully nonchalant word of thanks that nevertheless incorporated a subtle reiteration of the offer and confirmation that I accepted it.

'Maybe you should keep the NAAFI notepaper thing going one more time when you reply. But make it clear that, after that, all future correspondence should be sent to your people at home.'

'My *people*?'

'Your parents,' he amended, colouring slightly.

His days with us were numbered. Falling through the barrack room ceiling had convinced the CO that Henry was not the sort of man who would make an outstanding junior subaltern of infantry on any battlefield, nuclear or not. Knocking out his opponent in the first round at the boxing tournament proved no mitigation of circumstance either. He had hit Private Ball a millisecond after the bell for the first round, while Ball was still adjusting the waistband of his PT shorts. It was held – even by us – an unsporting thing to do. Henry, with his genial drawl and jug ears, his Petersen pipe and all his many anecdotes of the daily round in rural Norfolk, was being posted to the Intelligence Corps.

'I think I am supposed to feel ashamed,' he explained.

'But you don't.'

'Hardly. A change of scene is always welcome. And, taking a wider view, it's no bad thing to put blokes who can't stand the army into Intelligence. You don't want ambitious or energetic people messing things up. Short wars, that's the answer. Office hours and short wars.'

'Are you going to university, Henry?'

'I suppose I could,' he mused, not without a sly smile. 'Though look at the people they're letting in these days.' He patted me on the shoulder. 'Only joking.'

That was the thing of it: I *did* consider myself an impostor. My native accent was still unreconstructed lower-middle-class London, as compared to Henry's burbling

Received Pronunciation. He had been to places I knew nothing about, even though they existed in my own country. There was an uncle in Northumberland, for example, and not one but two aunts on the Isle of Wight. He owned things I had never seen before, such as monogrammed silver hairbrushes and a dark blue sponge bag that actually contained a sponge. He was, I considered, the real article.

'But then,' he objected, 'you are so amazingly anxious about everything that you'll go to University and do well and end up running the country.'

'You see me as anxious?'

'Twitchy.'

He thought about it some more, filling his Petersen with tobacco sent from home and lighting it with a luxurious flourish from an ancient brass lighter.

'Uncertain,' he settled on finally.

I wrote to my mother, telling her that whatever she did, she must keep any letter from Trinity safe and not bin it, or use it to light the boiler. Under no circumstances was she to show the envelope to my father. On the other hand, she could tell him that I was going before a War Office Selection Board in February, with a view to becoming an officer. Indeed, she could make of that as much as she liked.

There was leave at Christmas and I hitched home by various indirections, clumping up Eastfield Road in my ammunition boots, the greatcoat I was wearing heavy with rain. My father opened the door and studied me through a cloud of Capstan Full Strength. His first words were utterly predictable.

'Thank God we've got a Navy,' he said.

My mother had hidden the letter from Trinity in a saucepan and I recovered it during the first cup of tea we took alone.

'What does it mean?' she asked.

'I've got a place there to read English.'

'What I'm saying is, who's going to pay?'

'The British taxpayer.'

'Ha!' she snorted. 'I can see the kind of people you've been hanging out with. And your father's none too pleased about this officer business you told me to tell him about. He doesn't think you'll ever be an officer.'

'Tell him he can get knotted.'

'You tell him. He'll like that.'

But in the end it wasn't the idea of having a second officer in the house that distressed him but the offer from Trinity. Many years later, somebody wiser than me pointed out that he was a constitutionally jealous person. I suggested a better word might be envious, but the word jealousy carries with it a sexual charge that reflected his own history. Regarding university, I had in some way given myself to a secret lover, someone he would never meet.

'What does it tell you that you got in just by writing some silly scruffy letter?' he huffed. 'It tells me something.'

'And what's that?'

'They are having trouble making up the numbers.'

However, mentioning it around the office next day changed his mind a little. His colleagues were very impressed by Trinity's generosity. He came home with a different take.

'Of course, it's one of the biggest colleges, measured in numbers of students. That helped.'

'Yesterday you said they were making up the numbers.'

'I've got better things to think about,' he said, ending the argument.

S and her parents took a much more positive view of the way things had turned out in three short months. George had never come across the Suffolks on his march to the Rhine but knew people who spoke well of them. Wise bird that he was, he had also met enough childlike wartime subalterns to recognise the type in me.

'If they want to make you an officer,' he explained, 'you don't really have a lot of say in the matter. I should think you'll do very well, what with being tall and that.'

He was unconsciously echoing the sentiments of Alf, the Arnhem veteran, and, further afield, my uncle Jim. The night before I joined the army my father had taken me to Kentish Town to see his brother. Four pints and a couple of whiskys had seen me legless, throwing up into a garden hedge along the Seven Sisters Road.

'I think you're going to make a lovely little soldier,' Jim said, cradling my spinning head. 'You've got the hang of it already. Once you've got your knees brown, there'll be no stopping you.'

'Let me die,' I moaned.

'That comes later.'

About the offer from Trinity, S and I were careful to discuss it away from her house, for on this subject George and Vi maintained a confused silence. From their point of view and in purely class terms, I had done the impossible. People like us simply did not go to university, let alone one that we believed was set aside for toffs.

'Well, we always knew you was bright,' Vi admitted gamely. 'Anyone can see that.'

But what could be deduced from this perception was, as my grandfather would have put it, hanging on the old barbed wire. For Vi, it was not so much a story about me as about her daughter. A year had passed since we had first met and, in the unelaborate way there was of speaking of such things in those days, we were definitely 'going out'. Before I enlisted, I often joined S and her parents on Sunday drives around Epping and elsewhere, staring in wonder at big houses with rhododendrons, or tricksy cottages with some feature like a wagon wheel leaning against a whitewashed wall, or a sundial on the lawn. There was no spirit of envy in these explorations; it was just a way of registering another world that ran parallel to our own. We were modest and unassuming tourists, clocking this man's show of delphiniums; in another place, a well-sited dovecote or the fretted bargeboards to a garden shed.

'I bet the people in there must be important,' Vi would say.

'Now, what *are* you talking about, my dear?' her husband would counter, nursing the Hillman along leafy lanes.

'I'm just saying.'

I shared George's view that whoever they were, these people, they had little or nothing to do with me.

On this brief weekend leave, S and I moved from 'going out' to 'going steady', indicating an eventual exchange of vows. It seemed both romantic and inevitable to think this way.

We were nineteen. She had joined the commuter trains as a bank clerk in Barclays head office but one who read Iris Murdoch and went to see West End plays. Henry was shrewd to identify in me a social awkwardness that it took me many years to dispel (if I ever have) but S would have given him pause. Like him, she saw the world clear and whole. The deference that she had been taught as a child was growing irksome to her. The whole point of going out, going steady, was to have things our way.

On this leave, we ate an appalling meal at a self-styled Italian restaurant in Enfield, furtively totalling the bill and exchanging money under the table like dustmen eating at the Ritz. Once we were safely out in the street, S was majestical.

'We'll do better than that in the future, you'll see,' she said.

To passers-by, we were just two bits of kids who needed to grow up. I may have said as much. She gave me her grumpy frown.

'That is our money in that man's till,' she explained. 'Of

course we can do better than that rubbish. That's a promise. Tell me about Trinity.'

'I don't know what to say.'

'Good Lord,' she snorted. 'Only six months ago you were talking about applying to Reading. Surely you're pleased with yourself, for once.'

There was something tart in this last remark that gave me pause. Had I really spent my time with her moaning? It was natural that I should compare my own parents unfavourably with hers; but had I spoiled too many walks, too many moonlit trysts, by harping on about them?

'I am very pleased with myself,' I said. 'In fact, you are looking at a whole new person. From now on, I am going to make it my duty to be insufferable.'

'Won't take much,' she said.

I exercised my new personality by undoing her bra on the way home. Her expression was calm, even serene.

'Pigeon eyes,' she said, pushing me away.

I do not think any of the letters I wrote to her from this time have survived. They must have made dull reading, for I can remember trying too hard to say something literary. Did I actually send the letter that described sleet bouncing off the barracks window-panes at midnight or the moon seen through glass? It was the sort of poetic detail that makes paper curl. Her letters to me were reassuringly commonplace. They went into the breast pocket of my tunic and marched about with me on parade, or shared the bitter cold and damp of the rifle range. It was the army way. If you had a girl, you wrote to her. If she was a nice girl, she replied.

Before I left to hitch back to Bury St Edmunds, my father mounted a counter-barrage to my garbled account of the readiness of the armed services for nuclear war. In the event that Henry and his colleagues could not prevent the Russians heading for the Atlantic coast in newly irradiated tanks, he, Bert, had the task of squirrelling away the Government and other interested parties in deep underground bunkers. I asked him whether he had included himself in the lists of those chosen to survive.

'Me? I shall go down to Dover and take them on as they land.'

'You could show 'em your medals,' my mother suggested.

He pointed at me.

'You think Dolly Daydream here can hold them back?'

I tried a facetious note.

'Don't count on me. I shall be bunking off for west Wales and a small trawler, mate.'

Bert studied me without love in his eye.

'I bet you will,' he said.

The army saw things differently. The War Office Selection Board was a four-day affair that concentrated on skills of a kind not often employed in anything resembling the world of real events. Split into teams, we attempted to bridge muddy pits with a forty-gallon oil drum, a few bits of wood and unequal lengths of scaffolding pole. One frosty morning, in an individual test, we climbed to the top of a very tall tree and leaped for a rope dangling an enticing four or five feet away. Some candidates refused. When this happened, the officer sitting on a trembling bough nearby made furtive notes on his clipboard.

'Bad luck,' he said diplomatically.

To demonstrate the quality of mind required in a junior officer, we delivered lectures to each other on a variety of subjects that might attract the attention of the examiners. I remember one candidate gave a compelling account of the social history of whisky, which was much praised by a conducting officer with a face ravaged by his own research into the topic.

At the end of the course there was a one-on-one interview. I was shown into the presence of a major with a silly-ass moustache and a generous row of campaign medals. Whether he had ever found cause to jump out of a tree to clutch at a rope seemed doubtful; he was where he was because of a minor public school education and job vacancies created by the fortunes of war. A practised suavity filled his side of the desk.

'Know anything about wine?' he asked as his first question.

'Never drunk it, sir.'

'What's your favourite grub?'

'Shepherd's pie.'

'Good man,' he said admiringly. 'Cook it yourself, can you?'

There was a potential trap here: if I said yes, he might well ask whether I enjoyed needlepoint or had a boyfriend who played the violin. I temporised.

'It's the only thing I can cook.'

'Lucky blighter. The best shepherd's pie I ever ate was in Cairo.'

I waited for the punchline; there wasn't one. He drew a sheet of paper towards him.

'We'll just knock off these pro-forma questions. Has any member of your family ever held the Queen's Commission?'

'My father.'

'Good show,' he said, making a notation. 'Regiment?'

'The RAF.'

Sorrowfully, he scratched out what he had just written. We tried another tack.

'Rugby man?'

'Yes.'

'Greatest fly half in the world today?'

'Jackie Kyle.'

'Getting a bit elderly, isn't he?'

'Genius is ageless.'

He smiled and wrote vigorously for a few moments.

I passed these tests (though only those who fell out of the tree or lectured on the iron truths of Leninist-Stalinist philosophy, Diaghilev or Doris Day ever failed) and spent sixteen weeks on the Duke of Westminster's estate as an officer cadet. Just before being commissioned, I was invited to nominate the regiment of my choice. My first pick was the Royal Fusiliers, a sign of complete social ignorance that was treated as such. The second was the Somaliland Scouts and the third the King's African Rifles. This news delighted Uncle Jim.

'He has got himself fixed up with an African mob.'

'But he ain't black, is he?' his youngest son objected.

'No, mate, only his privates.'

I have been reminded of this sally at least once a year for the past half-century.

Newly commissioned officers had a clothing allowance of £74, with which they were supposed to buy patrols – mess uniform – and whatever other little outward signs of rank they fancied. Bert got me to sign this draft over to him and my mother went off to jumble sales to find a dinner jacket as a replacement. She came home with something that the great cornet player Bix Beiderbecke might have worn when playing hotel gigs in New Orleans thirty years earlier. Modelling it, I looked like a walk-on in some provincial rep.

'I am trying to make a good impression,' I wailed.

'Not everybody can look like George Raft.'

'I don't want to look like George Raft, either.'

'You'll get used to it,' she sighed.

She was speaking about her own life as much as mine. Time had wearied her and nowadays the fireworks had been replaced by a slow and melancholic mudslide. She was not yet fifty and, it seemed, was destined to grow old and die in Waltham Cross.

S and I spent our last evening together for sixteen months going to see the film *Gigi* in Leicester Square and then walking to Goodge Street, where coaches were waiting to take about 120 of us to Northolt, whence we would fly to Kenya, a country I had barely heard of in a continent of which I knew nothing.

'You'll write?' S asked.

'Every day,' I promised.

It was simple code, meaning will the relationship survive? The question was open-ended, for would it be the end of the world if it did not?

My brand-new uniform cap sat on my head like a dunce's and we were being watched by a couple of dozen service wives and their children, who were also included in the draft. They had the look of people concerned with a much more practical consideration: what was it like to get on a plane and trust to laws of physics never explained at school? Flying was for film stars. They did not feel like film stars.

S pecked me on the lips, turned and twinked away down the rainy pavements. The conducting officer came over to introduce himself, a breezy youth who looked as though he would be happier walking home from school. Looking at him, I saw myself. The army wives huddled together for company, their bare legs glistening with rain, their cigarettes dancing.

Chapter Four

IN 1954, NAIROBI WAS A CITY HARDLY FIFTY YEARS old. It had expanded from a railhead for the line running westwards from the coast. For many Europeans, its fertile soil and healthy climate soon made it a terminus. If Kenya was ever going to be a white man's country, this was the place from which to rule it. The fairly recent migration of tribes from the north and east made these high plains more densely peopled than elsewhere, though what claims or titles the Africans held could be dealt with by pen-pushers in the Colonial Office in the usual way. For white entrepreneurs, the land was more valuable by far than anywhere else along the track of the railway; and Nairobi's elevation provided, in addition to sweet air and a moderate climate, many a pleasing vista. Missionarising on a dead-flat plain in the east of the country, surrounded by thorn bushes and incurring the enmity of Arab neighbours who had until very recently been slave traders, was one thing. From a house or bungalow in the European style, built more than 5,000 feet above sea level, gazing at the sunrise racing across rolling plains was a very different experience. There was even a proper amount of rain.

Leaving all political and moral questions aside, Nairobi was one of the best-sited cities in the Empire. Barely a hundred miles to the north ran the equator – but as a light, airy notion and not the killing latitude that it is to the West. On paper, and especially in the prospectuses of European land agents, there could surely be nowhere finer to live in Africa than the swiftly dubbed White Highlands. This was Surrey with zebras. Half the minuscule white population of the entire country lived and worked in Nairobi itself, barely aware that in the past twenty years the African population had doubled. There were almost as many white people living in Kettering as there were in the whole of Kenya, overseeing the fortunes of more than 5 million Africans. The colony imported nearly twice as much as it exported and its principal client was an indulgent mother country. It was paradise running at a loss.

But the real rub lay in that grotesque imbalance of white over black. It seems so obvious now. In 1954 I had lived nineteen years without giving colonial despotism a single thought. All the evidence presented here for an inevitable human tragedy has been gathered by me after the event. I was on that plane from London as a romantic, a traveller into the unknown. The subaltern's pips on my shoulder were merely the price of the flight.

*

The road from the airport into Nairobi was lined with handsome grass verges. Beyond these were trees – in a better description, towering shrubs – screening run-down shacks. Their tin roofs blinked in the sunlight. Occasionally the view opened out to reveal a compound of mud huts where women sat in the shade watching their naked children run about among the dogs and chickens. As for those generous verges, we had not gone very far before we passed a truck jacked up on its rear axle by logs, surrounded by a crowd watching the driver wield a block of concrete as an improvised heavy hammer. A little further on were stalls of vegetables.

What took my eye in this first glimpse of Africa was the warm red of the soil and the luscious green of the vegetation. This was no arid landscape but a place rich, almost insolent, in its plenty. The air was scented with woodsmoke, aniseed, cattle piss and, every so often, black and sullen lakes of human waste. The people wandering the verges moved with that beguiling economy of effort that is the signature of life in all hot climates. I watched a girl break into a run, her body thrown forward from the hips, her actions the exaggerated parody of a long-distance runner at the end of her tether. After a few yards she came upright, laughing, and sauntered on.

I travelled this crowded road in the back of a one-ton truck, too shy – or too stupid – to sit with the driver. As we passed, clouds of rose-coloured dust swamped everyone on the road behind us, only those with the brightest clothes any longer visible. But there was a further telling detail. The engine note of a military vehicle is almost impossible to mistake, yet no one looked up, neither at our approach nor at our passing. I had arrived like many another youthful European before me, hungry for adventure, yet there was something even in that first hour or so that told me I was joining the story too late. In the past, it was the indigenous population that remained invisible, until summoned in the shape of a houseboy or room waiter, a laundress or gardener. Now the jig was up. In this whole fractious journey through the outskirts of Nairobi, I failed to make eye contact with a single person. Effectively, it was I who was not there – or, if I was, only as an irritating and faceless cloud of dust.

When I presented myself at the gates of Buller Camp, I was coated red from head to foot. It amused the guard commander but dismayed the orderly room staff to whom I was directed.

'You should have insisted on sitting up front,' a truculent officer barked from behind his desk. 'Just what I need, another romantic bloody schoolboy. Your lungs are probably already shot to buggery and you've only been here five minutes. But much more to the point, you're an officer. You *don't* ride in the back of a truck like a sack of onions. That should be obvious.'

Things had got off to an equally bad start at the airport. It was hot but not oppressively so and the sky through which I had so recently travelled was dotted with cotton-wool clouds, like an advertisment for soap powder. I wandered about for a few minutes on the pitted tarmac, peering into shadows, before finding a transport office. It was hardly more than a bare concrete box.

'Yes?' a corporal asked, over the edge of his paperback Mickey Spillane.

'I need to get to Uganda.'

'Oh yeah? And why is that?'

My subaltern's pips were making no impression.

'Because my unit is the 4th Ugandan Battalion, King's African Rifles.'

'And you feel like joining them, eh?' this corporal continued with the same practised insolence. But I was one of Sergeant Holyoake's graduates.

'Get up off your arse when speaking to an officer, you little turd.'

And he did, with elaborate slowness.

'You might find that when you look at your movement order more closely, you'll see 4 KAR is here. In Kenya. There's a bit of a war on. Sir.'

'A war?'

'A bit of a to-do. You're the officer. I expect you got your own words for it.'

If Buller Camp was the outward expression of this to-do, it was very laconic in the management of its affairs. I was shown to a tent, where a civilian batman, a boy in his teens, lay sleeping. He roused himself, smiled and disappeared under the braillings like a bolting pig. His job was to rob me blind, a thing he could not do until I had unpacked.

A few moments later, a plump and newly hatched subaltern with a flywhisk wandered in. He saw me staring at the whisk and made a few lacklustre swipes, forehand and backhand.

'Think it's too much? Somebody said I look like a Greek shopkeeper. But yesterday I actually *swallowed* a fly. About the size of a blackberry. I imagine they've put you on this Swahili course? Starts tomorrow.'

Denis was born to draw enemy fire. We sat next to each other at dinner that night and he began a ball-by-ball account of how he made eighty-seven runs for the school against the most bastard fast bowling ever encountered by the First XI. He had five runs to go before his unlucky dismissal when a general called out, 'Will someone tell that little pimple to shut up?'

'It's the boy with the flywhisk, sir.'

'Flywhisk? *Flywhisk?* What regiment?'

'2 KAR.'

'Good Christ,' the general bellowed. 'I would rather be a piano-player in an Egyptian brothel than an officer of 2 KAR. Or any other KAR.'

These pleasantries were flung down a table seating twenty-five on each side. The food was determinedly English. Denis hid his head over a plate of treacle pudding and custard, blushing to the roots of his hair.

'Bastard,' he said later, when we were back in the tented lines. We were drinking whisky at ten shillings a bottle and taking turns at despatching moths to the cover boundary. Denis, it turned out, had scored his runs batting seven – *seven* – and he would like to see that grim old bugger do as well, even half as well, what with the light as it was that day and the juice in the wicket.

'What do you know about prebendary deans?' he asked suddenly.

'Nothing.'

'My father's one.'

The Swahili course was conducted by a hugely amiable black warrant officer with grey hair. He taught me so well that two years later in Paris I conducted a one-sided conversation with a ticket clerk on the Metro before realising I was speaking the wrong language. Swahili has charm. We met in class every morning and afternoon, learning grammar and compiling vocabulary lists. At night we took a cab into Nairobi, generally to the New Stanley Long Bar, where it was said that, if one waited long enough, someone one knew from the other end of the earth would walk in. Denis supervised these forays. He drank gin to our bottles of Tusker beer and wore a daffodil-yellow tie. From time to time he would shoot his cuff and glance at an extremely expensive watch.

'We need to organise some women,' he was fond of muttering. Life in the cathedral close was now clearly nothing but a memory. He had a place to read classics at Wadham, 'By which time,' he promised, 'I shall be the most accomplished swordsman in Britain. I don't know what it is about me, I really don't, but girls go crazy in my presence.'

He was looking in the wrong place at the New Stanley. We lowered our sights a little and took to meeting at a Welcome Club run by the daughters of Nairobi notables. In this way I went to stay with the Vigars, whose son was a lieutenant in the Kenya Regiment and his sister Joan a volunteer at the Welcome. Mr Vigar was a placid-tempered man for whom young officers like me were no more vexing than puppies. He asked me where my battalion was and I told him: Fort Hall.

'On the doorstep of the Aberdares. Tremendous trout fishing up there. But I don't suppose you're going for that.'

'To tell you the truth, I don't really know what I'm doing in your country at all, sir.'

'That will change,' he promised. 'Your friend Denis says you are likely to pass top of the Swahili class.'

'*Denis* has been here?'

'A strange boy,' Mr Vigar said, after a delicate pause. 'Is it true his father is a clergyman?'

With Joan Vigar and another woman, Denis and I went to see *The Glenn Miller Story*, a further touch of surrealism in what seemed like an already crowded calendar. There were army trucks and plenty of uniforms to be seen on the streets of Nairobi but here we were, swanning about like coffee planters or sisal farmers, smoking Denis's Balkan Sobranies and – at his further insistence – drinking gin slings. After the film, Joan's nervy friend confided to me that she was the last person to have slept with the bandleader before his untimely death. We eyed each other speculatively.

'You lived in Cambridge,' I suggested, for that was where Miller kept rooms.

'God, no. In Knightsbridge. I was a Wren, at the Admiralty. That film has revived so many awful memories, I really can't ask you home,' she added, tears in her eyes, her bottom lip thrumming.

'Don't you see?' Denis agonised later. 'What she was actually saying was, take me home and roger me senseless. Didn't you at least get a telephone number?'

Some of the people we met at the New Stanley seemed more the genuine article, huge men with reddened cheeks and comfortable swags to their bellies, drinking Tuskers with concentrated deliberation, their hair stiff with dust. One such suggested we repair to the Travellers Club, of which he was not a member. We walked halfway up a flight of stairs, crashing from wall to wall, and were met by the owner, a woman in a black frock with a double loop of pearls. She was holding a tiny pistol.

'Shame on you,' she said to our civilian guide. 'These boys ought to be tucked up in bed.'

'Never mind that,' he said drunkenly. 'We're coming in.'

She raised the pistol.

'Get out of my club before I blow your head off.'

'You make a very telling argument, madam,' Denis fluted nervously. He patted the stranger on his beefy shoulder. 'Bob, I believe we are unwelcome.'

'She's talking to me, you little shit,' Bob shouted, rounding on us. We turned and fled into the night.

At the conclusion of the Swahili course I said my regretful goodbyes and set off by Land-Rover up-country, hammering along until brought up short by an amazing scene. Just south of the Blue Post Hotel in Thika, a platoon of white soldiers were firing into a small and flooded quarry by the side of the road, the bullets ripping up reeds and feathery grasses. Commanded by a captain in shorts, this hail of fire was directed at an invisible enemy that was surely already dead. But nobody was too anxious to put this to the test. The first man sent in was a loyal Kikuyu in a battered hat and army greatcoat, armed only with a panga. He disappeared from view for a while and then re-emerged, dragging a half-naked girl, smothered in blood but alive. My driver took the chewing stick from his mouth, spat out some pulp and waved me back to the vehicle. His expression was wooden.

'Mau Mau?'

He shrugged. In the shade thrown by the side of a bus, passengers sat looking at nothing in particular, their legs stuck straight out in front of them. The driver and his cronies were playing cards. They too had nothing to say.

Our destination was a requisitioned secondary school in Fort Hall, then hardly more than a trading post. The classrooms housed the headquarters company and was the fief of our extremely uncharismatic CO. The three rifle companies were ten miles away, each to its own ridge in the Aberdares. I was assigned to B Company but not before being invited to the sergeants' mess, where wicked old soldiers drank and watched movies projected on a sheet strung between two trees. It was considered wonderfully funny to show two films at once, mixing the reels and screening them in any order. While we junior officers necked down the beer and had halves of mingled spirits pressed upon us, about a hundred glum Ugandan soldiers, that I had to learn to call askaris, sat on the other side of the screen, piecing together a story that jumped from black and white to colour, from the sullen and sneering Richard Widmark with a gun in his hand to Cuddles Sakall, patting his hands together in mock despair. I ended the evening on my hands and knees, throwing up what seemed like every ounce of food I had ever eaten.

'You are now ready for battle, sir,' the signals sergeant said in a kindly way, ruffling my hair. 'It has been a pleasure meeting you. Your company sergeant major up there will be Wally Cooper, a fund of sound advice on military matters.'

In the morning, more dead than alive, I consulted the armourer and drew a M1 Garand, an American weapon that had the advantage of being self-loading. I asked him how much ammunition I would need.

'Put it this way. It's not Omaha Beach.'

I picked up the Garrand almost casually without realising that for the next sixteen months it would scarcely be out of my reach. Just before midday, a Land-Rover arrived, driven by an askari three or four inches taller than me and at least two stone heavier. He flung my bedding roll into the back, along with two huge boxes of tinned beef, not before opening each and fishing out a green and pink certificate issued by the Sultan of Dar es Salaam, confirming that the meat had been butchered in the appropriate manner. It seemed a good time to try out my Swahili. *What's your name? How far is it to B Company? Has there been any fighting recently?* The driver looked at me with half a smile, blew his nose on his fingers and, like a monk sworn to silence, indicated the front seat. We left the compound doing forty in third gear. I gave up any attempt at conversation and rolled us each a cigarette. Africa spooled past.

B Company had made itself comfortable a few hundred yards from the treeline of the Aberdare Mountains and next door to a Kenya Police post, manned by two indolent blonds. Their camp and ours was surrounded by barbed wire and sharpened bamboo stakes. The army taste for studied eccentricity was indicated by a mud-and-wattle mess hut with a corrugated tin roof, where I found Major Campbell; another subaltern, originally from the Gordon Highlanders; a nondescript captain whose job it was to amuse Campbell; and Sergeant Major Cooper.

Campbell was a collector's item: brusque, highly opinion-ated and, as he took care to tell me in his speech of welcome, a soldier's soldier. Once, his kind had policed the Empire, peppering the natives with insults and reserving to itself a sort of muddy omniscience.

'If you can get even one of these buggers to sight and fire a rifle in the correct way, you'll have done well,' he told me.

His own markmanship was exhibited that same evening. While we sat inside the mess hut listening to the rain lashing down, Campbell drew his pistol and amused himself by firing holes in the roof immediately above our heads. Sergeant Major Cooper sat with his shoulders hunched, silvery little gouts falling onto his balding head and onto the pad of blue airmail paper on which he was laboriously scratching a letter to his wife.

'Take some water with it, Sergeant Major,' Campbell called. This was considered a Wildean jest by his second-in-command, another Bob, his nose in a tumbler of whisky. What everyone called sausage flies smashed into the pressure lamps. Moths with wings as big as toffee papers littered the table.

'Go and inspect the guard, someone,' Campbell muttered, bored.

'A fine soldier,' the Gordon Highlander subaltern explained later. We shared a tent pitched over a deep rectangular trench, the better to offer headroom. The Scot had the advantage of me because he owned a torch. While I stumbled about, falling over things, he on his side of the tent stripped naked and, with his back turned, did arm-swinging exercises before slipping into his bedding like a letter posted through the front door. The moment this happened, the torch was switched off.

'Never let your men see you at a disadvantage,' he advised in the dark.

'How is that most likely to happen?'

'For example, never let them see you naked.'

I fell asleep trying to imagine under what circumstances this might come about – or where and when it had happened to him.

It annoys me now that I cannot remember the name of this man, for he too was an army cliché. Everything he said about his background suggested castles and deer-hunting, the laird's annual ball and a roomful of sporting guns, though Cooper later confirmed my suspicions. He was not the pattern hero of the film *The Hasty Heart* but the son of a small-town auctioneer and, in Cooper's opinion, 'a bit of a three-pound note to anyone who's had any dealings with the real Jocks'.

Put upon, out of his element, the sergeant major was looking for an ally and searched for it in me.

'See, you have got the lingo off pat, whereas I can't string more'n a couple of words together. The major would sooner clean his teeth with dogshit than give it the old Swahili and the captain is nothing more than a poor lost soul who ought to be wearing carpet slippers.'

'Are you sure you should be telling me all this, Sergeant Major?'

'I am telling you for your own effing benefit, sir, and I hope in doing so I have given no offence. These buggers – the Mau Mau, I mean – are ruthless little sods and if they ever get among us we shall have all on. And I mean all on.'

It was Cooper who had supervised the construction of the camp's defences, which were elaborate enough to repel an attack measured in hundreds. In quiet times he would add a further circle of razor-sharp bamboo to the perimeter, laced with tripwires attached to tin cans half filled with pebbles.

Two days after my arrival, I went to ambush a bridge in the valley below, slipping and sliding down a precipitous path in total darkness. We were, as the manual would phrase it, in section strength, the askaris who accompanied me showing a nonchalant disdain for the whole idea. We lay out overlooking a bridge that I could not myself see and waited for something to happen that I could not easily imagine. About three in the morning, without a word of command from me, my section, some of whom had served in Burma during the war, began firing. We put up a parachute flare and what had been velvety nothing was suddenly revealed as a scene of wild confusion, as nearly a hundred young women dropped their loads and bundles and ran about screaming.

The firefight seemed to last a quarter of an hour but was probably over in minutes. By the last flare, we could see that the bridge and surrounding area were deserted, save for the sacks and wicker baskets that the women had been carrying. Mercifully, we had missed every single one of the porters.

'We will stay and see whether anyone comes back to collect the food,' I ordered uncertainly.

The soldier next to me jerked up his chin, eloquently indicating that anyone with any sense would by now be far, far away.

The following morning I consulted Cooper and found that eight men had fired 117 rounds and 4 mortar bombs, 3 of them flares, all aimed at a gaggle of women. This I reported to Campbell.

'It was a poor show,' he snapped, 'utterly lacking in the killer instinct.'

'The women were unarmed and unaccompanied.'

'Says you. Wait for me in the Land-Rover.'

We drove to a palisaded village a mile or so away down the ridge and were admitted by half a dozen armed elderly men wearing red brassards. The headman presented himself and listened impassively to Campbell's harangue, conducted in English.

'Last night, some of your young ladies attempted to go up the mountain and give food and succour to our friends in the forest. Don't shake your head at me, you insolent bugger, you know I am speaking the truth. If I ever catch one of them, I will have their guts for garters. I will nail their ears to a tree.'

The headman turned his head towards me, his eyes thick with a milky-blue film. Most of the teeth in his head had gone missing long ago. The hand that held his panga, a little sword of beaten iron, was corded with veins.

'What is this child doing here?' he asked in Swahili.

'What'd he say?' Campbell barked. 'Repeat those words to me.'

'He says he understands.'

In the four-year campaign against the Mau Mau, fewer than a hundred whites were murdered but 10,000 Africans lost their lives. The people we talked to that morning were victims on both sides of the argument. Their original homes, little huts in a fold of the land, connected to their neighbours' land by the threads of goat-tracks, now lay abandoned. In their place was this defended and entirely artificial 'village', the creation of some unknowable white mind. Guarded by a few men with ancient shotguns and further protected by an electrically discharged maroon that they were only to let off in face of all-out attack, people who had once lived and roamed over hundreds of acres were now herded together under a military regime.

On the other hand, everyone knew that the Mau Mau would destroy cattle by the cruellest method possible, by cutting off the front legs, or disembowelling the poor beasts. Innocents who refused them food or shelter were despatched in the same brutal way. Much more than any white man, the people in that village knew the full meaning of the administered oath that bound the terrorists together. The climate of fear that hung over white Nairobi was to a great extent fed by hysteria: stories of house servants suborned, gardeners mysteriously gone missing, family cars that had run like sewing machines suddenly immobilised. But this seldom led to all-out acts of terror. Up-country, the threat was much more real. A week after Campbell's threatening harangue, half the village we had visited went up in flames. Oily rags had been lit and tossed into the compound – but by how many men? Ten? Fifty? Sergeant Major Angadubu, one of the Burma veterans in the company, had a more plausible explanation.

'If somebody throws fire into your village, it is easy to kill the flames. Maybe one hut is destroyed. But here we see many huts burned.'

'What does it mean?'

Angadubu shrugged.

'The people want to please the soldiers but they also want to please the Mau Mau.'

'You think the fire was deliberately spread?'

'I think so,' he said, pursing his lips. His habit of examining the world with a frown on his face made him disliked by the other askaris, though I found it very appealing. Given even the simplest order – say, for mustering the men on parade – the sergeant major would bow his head in thought for a moment, as if reviewing every conceivable outcome, before looking me in the eye and giving a doubtful nod.

The undisputed clown of the platoon was one Sergeant Idi Amin, vain, bombastic and knuckleheaded. I can claim – or confess – to some small part in his future career. He asked whether if I could coach him in his English exam, by which he meant (though I was too innocent to see what he was talking about), could I fix the results? Amin was exceptionally good-looking and built along the lines of a light heavyweight boxer. In front of his men he loved to rant and threaten but towards Europeans he employed a wheedling, almost joshing tone. Unlike the cautious and avuncular Angadubu, if you gave Sergeant Idi Amin an order, he would sprint off with only half the business understood.

'If you want my advice, sir,' Wally Cooper said gloomily, 'I would always make that bugger walk in front when you're out on patrol.'

'You think he's impetuous?'

'I think he's exactly the bloke you don't want behind you with a loaded Sten,' Cooper confirmed. 'I see the English badge you got him has been sewn on back to front.'

I checked; it was true.

At some time in the past, B Company had stirred itself to create a forward base a mile or so into the forest. It was called, with a nod to military history, Fort William. The approach was along the spine of the ridge and the forest had been felled to create a roadway of sorts. Some noble hardwood trees lined the route, their branches noisy with colobus monkeys; but what gave the scene its character were enormous banks of bamboo, only occasionally cut by tracks, none of them wider than a small animal's hips.

Fort William was a forsaken clearing on a spur of the

ridge. I was no strategist but, even to my eye, the place had no purpose. An impenetrable wall of bamboo surrounded it and the weapon pits that had been dug were crumbling. There were recent animal tracks everywhere but no sign of human passage. For something to do, I ordered that we lay out in silence for a while, listening to the wind rustle in the tops of the forest. The experience was completely unnerving. It was as though our presence was an intrusion on some aboriginal emptiness – an elevated thought that came direct from books and examination halls. But then, Angadubu slowly held up his hand. Down on the valley floor, disguised by the breeze to sound much closer, we heard voices.

Angadubu smiled. He pointed to the virgin bamboo in front of us, the stems packed so closely together that only a rat could make its way. The voices stopped. There was a solitary and distant clunk as a panga bit into a stem and then, most eerie of all, a snatch of giggling laughter.

'Is there nothing we can do?' I whispered.

'No,' he said, patting me gently on the back.

I would have made a very unhappy subaltern in any other posting. Swanking about some town in Germany and caring for thirty or so disaffected and bored British soldiers would soon have found me out. Inter-platoon cricket in, say, Paderborn, was the path I might so easily have trodden – that, coupled with the invitation to be (at least in the evenings and over the mess silver) a gentleman as well as a conscript. For as long as I had been a private soldier I was kept up to the mark in appearance and behaviour by others. But I had few innate officer qualities and the demands made on my gentlemanly status had been confusing. At Grosvenor Hall, where I did my officer cadet training, when dressed in mufti we were required to walk about in rubberised mackintoshes and grey trilbies. Accordingly, on most Saturday afternoons in Chester, the pavements were clogged with faintly desperate young men with the appearance of underachieving rent collectors, or God-bothering Bible salesmen.

Even a few weeks in the shadow of the Aberdares had overturned all that attempt at social engineering, along with it my sketchy grasp of military law, notes on the proper care of soldiers' feet and how to address a letter to the colonel's lady in response to an invitation to make up the numbers at tennis. Sartorially, certainly, I was a different man now, a cross between a Montana cowboy and an East European pig farmer. I wore French paratrooper's trousers tucked into American army-surplus canvas boots. A camouflage smock was like a second shirt and on my head I wore a floppy linen hat to which Idi Amin had contributed a whimsical grey feather. I had an acid smell, from sleeping underground and for want of anything bigger than a canvas bucket to wash in.

S's letters came up by ration truck maybe once a week. In England it was summer and she was learning to play tennis on some municipal courts along the Enfield Highway. George was in the high season of Scout fêtes and jamborees; Vi had sprained her wrist. The next-door neighbours were planning to go to Paignton for their holidays. My letters back were far less easy and open in tone. There was a paradox here: more to say meant more strangled ways of saying it. I was in effect self-censoring. I was looking at the wrong things: Cooper's unconscious habit of fondling his balls while writing to his missus, Angadubu's stricken expression when arguing with Idi Amin. There were only so many ways of rhapsodising about a sunset, or describing the moods of the forest.

In Campbell's little mess we only ever ate one thing: curried chicken. By the time I arrived, the cook had got to the limits of this dish, concocting chicken so steeped in spice it was barely edible. Three bottles of Tusker to each place setting were there to help repair the damage done to our tongues and throats. The meal was finished off with a second Campbell-inspired delicacy: processed cheese, sent up from Nairobi in huge tins with a six-inch diameter. This was cut into generous roundels and served with strawberry jam, in the manner of an open sandwich. I quickly learned to follow Cooper's example, licking the jam from the cheese and masticating it hungrily to restore feeling to my mouth. Campbell, his eyes watering, would assume an easy nonchalance with the unchanging diet, spoiled only by shifting a buttock now and again to release a poisonous trumpet fart.

These nightly scenes, although intended to underline our quirky adherence to the officer code, only emphasised how far short we fell of civilised behaviour. Campbell himself was good-looking in a raffish sort of way and always came to the table with his tunic starched as crisp as wrapping paper, his medal ribbons prominent. But Cooper was right about Captain Bob, who shambled in, sometimes wearing a fringed paisley scarf around his neck, sometimes with blobs of shaving cream still decorating his earlobes.

Campbell was fond of anecdotes of Germany immediately postwar, when you could buy a woman for a handful of cigarettes, and a smart quartermaster could, by amassing the exact dead weight of a truck in scrap metal, have the whole bang shoot compressed into a couple of suggestive but nondescript cubes and so end up with ostensibly two trucks, one for him to dispose of as he wished. By contrast, Bob's gently rambling stories were all about women he'd met in shady English hotels with a direct line to flat-racing scoops.

'Not tarts, you understand, but properly horsey English ladies. Take, for example, Airborne,' he smiled. 'Has there been a bigger turn-up for the book in recent times?'

'Were you on it, sir?' Cooper asked dutifully.

'Was I ever? A Derby Winner at 50/1? Had I been able to scrape together a hundred quid—'

'Hah!' Campbell snorted.

'—I would have left the army toot sweet. As it was—'
He caught Campbell Effendi's eye and fell silent.

Most nights we played poker. Campbell – perhaps in a desire to rein in his second-in-command – would not permit gambling for money so we fell to betting in cigarettes. There was at the time an overseas brand of Players called Clipper, presented in a neat flip-top carton, twenty-five to a box. Cooper was the most hopeless poker player ever to sit at a table (characteristically, he expected to lose) and Bob would have given the teenage Thackeray points in recklessness. The Gordon Highlander liked to play the mathematical odds. But the ghost of my grandfather sat at my elbow. Lessons learned in brag or nap in Lambeth Walk proved their usefulness halfway up a mountain, 7,000 feet above sea level.

'Ten boxes.'

'Your ten and raise you ten.'

The biggest single bet was between me and Bob, when he wagered 25,000 cigarettes on a hand of three sevens. In my own hand I held a diamond flush. I gave my winnings to my platoon and ordered a pipe from a NAAFI catalogue, along with five tins of Three Nuns. I was so sick of chain-smoking tailored cigarettes that I have never bought a packet since. (Much later, when Campbell banned poker and the supply of free Clippers dried up, many in my platoon took up the pipe, so that we sat around in the forest like C. S. Lewis and the Inklings in the back bar of the Eagle and Child in Oxford; or perhaps some more silent coterie, say, of Arctic explorers adrift on the ice.)

Campbell had acquired a four-inch mortar that we occasionally pooped off in the general direction of the forest, always late at night and nearly always when we were drunk. The askaris watched from their tents, too well mannered, it sometimes seemed to me, not to pluck us out of the mortar trench and punch our lights out for the bumptious idiots that we were.

'You didn't stay for the fireworks last night, Sergeant Major?'

'I hope I got more self-respect,' Cooper muttered. He sat at his folding table, making out his ration indents, the papers held down by little pebbles.

'Pretty stupid thing to do, eh?'

'You know why I'm here, sir, seconded to this bloody shower? Dosh. And not a lot more than I'd have as a colour sergeant back home. But a few shillings extra. Whereas you—'

'Yes?'

Cooper jabbed his pen into the jug of black ink in front of him.

'I wouldn't like to say, sir,' he muttered.

It was the only real wound I suffered in the whole of the time I spent in Kenya. I shambled away and sat staring at the forest, the breeze plucking at my smock. Someone nearby was playing a little three-note piano, the keys made from flattened bicycle spokes, the case an ancient cigar box.

Chapter Five

ONLY ON THE HIGHEST REACHES OF THE ABERDARE bamboo forest was there anything like an open space and that seldom more than a few square yards of rain-flattened grass and desolate fern. From such a vantage it was possible to look down into the valleys on either side, where grey clouds moped, blind and disconsolate. The default image of patrolling that I have is of huffing and puffing about inside these clouds, soaked to the skin and dizzy with exhaustion. Once in a while, the track we followed would cross another and then – if we were lucky – we might crouch, staring at a human footprint, the heel filled with a tiny iridescent lake of rainwater, a sign that someone had passed this way a day or so earlier.

Whenever this happened, the arts of soldiering inculcated in England flooded back, displacing the more normal sensation I had of being a lost child in a fairy tale of half-lit woods. From now on we moved with inching caution, our breath seemingly as noisy as shunting engines, the faintest clink of equipment drawing reproving looks. Maybe our quarry was around the very next bend, hopefully with nothing more than a panga in his hand, but perhaps levelling a monstrous elephant rifle or a Czech-made sub-machine gun. (The first time I ever saw the latter, only later adopted by the British army, was when it was fired at me the length of an average suburban garden by a spectral figure in an old coat, a colobus skin on his head. I had plenty of time to reflect on my short life while waiting to be cut in half, but the Mau Mau was as startled at the meeting as I was, and the bullets only chopped bamboo a foot above my head.)

Anyone found in the forest was a shoot-to-kill target. It was a measure reinforced by constant warnings to the up-rooted farmers of the open spaces below. Into the treeline, the entire Aberdare range was a prohibited zone. And indeed, nobody in their right mind would willingly suffer its miseries. No tribe had ever lived there. Just once in a while we might find an improvised shelter with the sticky remains of a fire in front of it, weeks and sometimes months old. Such places were always temporary affairs, a stopover maybe, or a one-day fever hospital. In one shelter we found a crumpled red shirt, colonised by a seething army of ants; in another, the handle but not the tines of a Mappin & Webb dinner fork.

There was no horizon in the forest further than a dozen or so yards. It was common to pass a day dragging ourselves up almost vertical grey-green slopes, the only additional colour a yellow leaf borne along by sluicing rain, or the red filaments of frantic worms. There was no wind to speak of and the cloud that enveloped us seemed to hang like listless curtains, or, as it occurred to me one afternoon of semi-hallucinating exhaustion, wardrobes of old clothes: shrouds and milkmaid's smocks, nightgowns, coachmen's capes.

Eight or nine soldiers constituted a patrol. Idi Amin was far too fly to put himself forward for such unappealing duty, though I was amused to read in one of his obituaries that he must be credited with the invention and supervision of the entire patrol strategy. Sergeant Major Angadubu was loath to let me wander about without his mothering guidance but I thought of him as too old for the task. I put my trust in Abbassi, a surly young corporal with enough common sense for an entire regiment and an unequalled sense of direction. Though I carried a prismatic compass, I never once took it out of my pocket. Unfailingly, guided by senses that it seemed Europeans lacked, he led us out of the forest within a yard of where we had walked in.

Patrols lasted from three to five days. We ate bully beef and rice, though if we were near a river I would fish for trout with a few metres of line and a lure made from silver paper or threads from my shirt. Once the great men of the world had fished the lower reaches of these mountain rivers in knickerbocker suits and hobnailed boots, presumably with wallets of flies and the best Hardy rods. The fish knew nothing of this ancient history and practically hurled themselves onto the hook. On such nights we would eat like the most pampered clients of the New Stanley Hotel.

We spent some wonderfully unsoldierly evenings fuelled with rum, sobbing with suppressed laughter at the character assassination of a sergeant long dead, or the sexual foibles of British officers now safely tucked up in Tudor villas, reading the county cricket scores. Corporal Abbassi permitted all this levity up to a point but then would suddenly switch the conversation into Acholi, of which language I had not a word. It was a form of censorship that he enjoyed using. There were two occasions that I remember particularly well. The first was when a thigh-slapping account of how Idi Amin had volunteered for the regimental pipe band in order to get his hands on a Black Watch bonnet was finally squelched, just before the punchline. Likewise I recall the very abrupt change of subject when one of the younger soldiers asked me with feigned innocence why white men smelled so bad.

Wally Cooper listened to stories about life up the hill with a pouting lower lip.

'Nothing on earth would get me ten yards inside that bloody forest and that's no lie. You've heard of arthuritis, I take it. Not taking your boots off for days, getting into your pit at night soaked through: you'll be lucky to walk without two sticks by the time you're thirty.'

It *was* an unhealthy occupation, the more so for the askaris, muscled like art-school models but decidedly rheumy in the early morning. Unbidden and illicitly, Wally had started to include in his rations indent cough linctus for my platoon. He issued it with strict instructions never to let Campbell see the bottles.

'If the major asks you how you come by it, you just cop a deaf 'un, *comprendre?*' he would adjure some genial askari without a word of English, before passing the linctus across.

'What was your happiest time in the army, Sergeant Major?' I asked him once.

'Greece,' he replied instantly. 'Just after the war. I had charge of the stores at the time and you could sell them Greeks anything – *anything*. I hooked up with a brothel-keeper, nice bloke, nothing poncey, and we had a great little business going.'

Wally Cooper was a Shakespearean soldier, a fit companion for Bardolph, Pistol and Nym, and cut from the same ancient cloth. His job, as he explained it, was to be buggered about, morning, noon and night, by the army but always with something on the side for himself.

'Here's a such-as. I bet when you was a mere squaddie, you used to skive about with a clipboard, having a crafty smoke here and there behind the barrack blocks. Then when the officer of the day come along to ask what you was at, you'd tuck the clipboard under your arm, fling him a top-of-the-range salute and shout you was just off to see the Sergeant Cook, or whatever. Eh? Well, I invented that little number. I used to sell the boys a bit of three-ply and a bulldog clip and, my oath, soon enough the bloody lines were filled with soldiers – dozens of them – who were just off somewhere else. What the poet calls a hive of activity,' he added indulgently.

One morning we were having a companionable smoke when we saw a small convoy of Land-Rovers coming up the hill at breakneck speed. Campbell was immaculately dressed at all hours of the day but Wally and I dived into our tents to change shirts and tidy up while the gate guard (commanded inevitably by Idi Amin) received our surprise guest. He was General Sir George Erskine, the Commander in Chief. I sidled into the mess hut as he and Campbell were exchanging jolly-good-show banter over massive tumblers of gin.

'And, ah, do you find this a better place than Egypt, sir?' Campbell asked, referring adroitly to the general's most recent command. Erskine looked around the hut in elaborate panto-mime.

'I've seen slightly better digs up there, you know. Built more in the traditional style and so forth.'

This was considered convulsingly witty. The general was offered and accepted a roundel of cheese and strawberry jam, which he nibbled at with practised aplomb, a cigarette in his spare hand.

'Whose face is that at the window?'

'Sergeant Amin, sir,' Campbell cried in anguish, where Idi's grinning head wagged like a Punch and Judy puppet. He was waved away, but not before delivering a salute.

'Good morning, General, sah! Yes, sah!'

Erskine had begun to look thoughtful. His eye fell on me.

'You're the fellow who does all the patrolling, I take it?'

'Yessir.'

'Caught any of the blighters, have you?'

'Not too many. Well, none.'

'Why is that? Can we see a map?'

One was fetched and we bent our heads over it.

'Now, which are the principal routes taken by the Mau Mau? Show me the tracks you are covering on a regular basis. Dot in your ambush points and so forth.'

He was being perfectly serious. I mumbled away for a few minutes, pointing out that in very few places was there a path wider than a man's hips; that the Mau Mau – at any rate in our sector – were to be numbered in single figures; that contact was very often accidental, as of two men meeting in a dark alley. Erskine studied me with unswerving calm.

'These women we read about in the sitreps, the ones who resupply the little bastards, aren't they usually to be numbered in scores? And if so, where's all that food going? Are they simply feeding the ducks, is that what you're telling me?'

'I think it likely that if there *is* a organised command in the forest, they arrange to meet the women at full strength once in a blue moon – and that very briefly.'

'But you don't know.'

'Nobody does.'

Erskine's aide-de-camp looked sour but he, after staring me in the face for half a minute, smiled.

'You haven't got a drink,' he observed pleasantly.

All this while, Wally Cooper had been standing at ease in parade-ground style, his belt more or less cinching enormous shorts, his chin out. Campbell nodded that he too could serve himself a drink, which he did by pouring a bottle of Tusker into a pint glass. This he sipped at, as dainty as a duchess.

'You know who I blame most for the way things are going?' Erskine burst out suddenly. 'The Governor-General.'

He wheeled round.

'What do *you* make of the Governor-General, Sergeant Major?'

Wally stiffened, his glass halfway to his lips.

'The Governor-General, sir? *The Governor-General?* Dia-fucking-bolical!'

'Just so,' Erskine murmured.

He knew more than he had let on. Had he told me that intelligence estimates of the number of Mau Mau holed up in the Aberdares and on Mount Kenya approached 5,000, even at this stage of the game, I would have disbelieved him. Had he told me that plans were in train to dig moats and fifteen-foot-high fences the length of the forest margins, interdicting the Aberdares to any new recruits or fleeing sympathisers, I would have been struck dumb with amazement.

A week after Erskine's visit, we picked up the track of a naked foot and followed it for six and a half hours, moving ever higher up the valley. In one place a palm print on a bamboo stem was so fresh that Corporal Abbassi could wipe his thumb across the film of mud and obliterate it. We cocked our weapons, huddled together like conspirators in an opera. I found myself listening – really listening – for the first time in my life. Sounds I had never before heard came flooding in, like the faintest swish of bamboo fronds high above our heads and even the rainwater running in tiny streams past my feet. We moved, we listened. Abbassi fished for a smile that came out as a baring of teeth. Jerking up his chin, he mimed sniffing. Though I could smell nothing, the rest of the patrol exchanged glances.

Half an hour later we broke out of a bamboo thicket in front of three caves, fifty yards away on the far side of a shallow ravine. We sank to the ground, amazed. In front of the caves burned a huge bonfire and round it were stakes that held drying clothes. It was a little like stumbling across a Lost City, for never had any of us imagined a camp of such size and domesticity. There were no guards and from the interior of the caves we could hear perfectly normally pitched conversation.

I had grown up watching war films and now found myself in the starring role. I knew what John Wayne's Sergeant Stryker would do but had no idea what to do myself. As we studied the ground, looking for a way to cross the ravine unobserved, a man wandered out from one of the caves, stark naked except for a battered brimmed hat. He was smoking a tiny stub of a pipe and held in his hands loops of mauve and grey animal intestine. His skin was coated in ash. He took a few steps and then froze, his body telling him something that his mind was struggling to acknowledge. He turned his head gently from side to side, and the guts he was holding slipped to the ground. What he was trying to process was that fifty yards away I was looking at him down the barrel of a Garrand rifle. It was one of the most intimate and unsettling moments of my life.

Then, with a bound, like an alerted deer, he turned on his heel and ran back into the cave.

There began, on our side, a frenzy of firing. After a minute or so of madness, about thirty similarly naked men and women burst out of the cave, jerking, skipping, loosing off rounds from home-made rifles and sporting guns, even a bow and arrow. And then they were gone, drifting into the surrounding forest like smoke. The pursuing bursts from our Bren gun chewed up slivers of bamboo that flew in arcs, like Indian clubs in a variety act. I stood up, dazed. The bonfire crackled, the clothes hung on their poles; otherwise the scene was empty.

There was blood on the ground in front of the caves but no bodies. We recovered piles of grubby typed paper, school exercise books stuffed with names, some of them ominously crossed out, a few miserable enamel plates and cups, and a handful of discarded weapons. At the very back of the cave, hidden under a scrap of cloth, I dragged out a Remington typewriter with splayed keys. On the ground near by was a peaked cap such as a park keeper might wear. When I came back out into the air, Corporal Abbassi was sitting on the ground smoking a cigarette. He looked unruffled, careless even. His smile was faint but curt.

'They move like birds,' he murmured. It was all the same to him whether we had mortally wounded anyone or not but I could see in his eye that he had registered my horror at having been put to the test. There was no judgement in his glance; he was a professional soldier with many years to serve, here on this mountain or anywhere else he was sent. I was, however respectfully he might phrase it, a supernumerary. Not a cowardly one, but no John Wayne either.

'D'you think we should look for the one we wounded?' I asked.

'It was a woman,' he said. 'A girl. We can follow her, if you like.'

To show his choice in the matter, he glanced at the sky or, more realistically, the quality of the light. It would be dark in four hours. I thought he was going to add something but he stood up in one fluent action and wandered away.

We burned all the clothes and scraps of bedding, skewered the plates and mugs with bayonets and flung them into the ravine, broke the stocks from the rifles we had recovered and threw the bolts as far as we could over the tops of the encircling bamboo. I thought about the Remington for a while and then crammed it into my Bergen rucksack. We divided the mounds of paper, swigged down the last of our water – and walked out.

*

On Christmas Day 1954, I was playing football with a biscuit tin stuffed with grass when an edge caught my shin and opened up a slashing cut. Four days later, my leg had swollen like a bolster from the ankle to the groin. I was lucky that on this particular patrol I had Angadubu with me. He improvised a stretcher and I was carried out, delirious. Campbell was on leave; Wally Cooper drove me to a field hospital staffed by bored young girls who turned out to be commissioned QARANC nurses.

'Don't you have showers up there?' one of them asked, disgusted, cutting me out of my clothes.

'Now then, sir,' Cooper whispered, 'don't get the hump. Just come it the Jungle Jim for a bit and you're on a promise here. Never mind Flossie,' he added, indicating the blonde who had wrinkled her nose at me. 'Pick a fat one out, say, her over there with the funny teeth. And don't hurry back.'

I was operated on while under the influence of penthathol, a drug that induced a most wonderful purple picture show and, it seemed, an extensive confessional monologue.

'You dirty little tyke,' the fat nurse with the funny teeth said cheerfully when I came round.

I was discharged from her care to a week's convalescent leave in Mombasa, travelling on the midday train from Nairobi in the company of an elderly couple who had recently sold up their farm in the White Highlands. Two hours into the journey we were all blind drunk. Hughie, who much resembled the actor Trevor Howard, wanted to know why we hadn't killed more Mau Mau, when the bloody forest was stuffed with them.

'Can't be that difficult. They don't know any more about living in the bamboo than you do. They're farmers.'

'And schoolteachers,' Hughie's wife put in, as though bracketing this profession with satanists and cannibals.

It was their opinion that white regiments would put up a better show and, nettled, I told them about the only death I had witnessed on our side. Meeting up with a detachment of the Inniskillings a month or so earlier, we had collaborated in hacking out a dropping zone for resupply by air. As the Piper Pacer circled and threw out its first sack of provisions, a fusilier stripped to the waist had run forward with the cry 'I've got it!' and attempted to catch a hundredweight of bully beef falling towards him at eighty miles an hour. He was killed instantly. Mrs Hughie wiped her mouth with the back of her hand.

'Brave boy,' she muttered.

On the last but one day of my leave I was taking tea on the terrace of the George V Hotel, Mombasa, when I was picked up by an indulgent and good-natured woman sailing home the next day. She told me her surname.

'Do you know anyone called that? I take it you're in the army.'

'The brigadier has the same name.'

'Well, there you are then,' she smiled.

We lay in whiter-than-white sheets, her well-fed plumpness next to the skin and bones that I had become in my brief career as Jungle Jim. What I liked best about her – but have never been able to emulate – was her reckless insouciance with hotel rooms. The floor was littered with her clothes and mine; her half-packed suitcases yawned like hippos. Long before it got dark we had called room service five times. We lay at either end of the bath, drinking champagne and singing Cole Porter numbers.

'I suppose you're going to go off to university somewhere and be fearfully brainy.'

'I shall certainly buy a duffle coat,' I promised.

'Well, I shall go back to Wiltshire and learn to be a grim old bag.'

'It's more likely you'll drive some man crazy.'

She laughed.

'That, chum, is a story about men, not me. Hop out and get dressed. My husband's coming down tonight to see me off.'

I sat up in the bath, surging the water over its edge.

'Your husband?'

'Be a dear and get them to take all the trays away. Oh, and perhaps someone to make the bed. And if you can bring my cigs in here before you let yourself out, that would be nice.'

She let me kiss her one last time and then stretched her arms above her head.

'What a nice way to remember Mombasa. I think I shall steal an ashtray.'

*

Soon after I returned to duty, we left the forest and were deployed in country that was the cliché of film-makers: tawny plains dotted with flat-topped wait-a-bit thorns, huge sunrises, roaming game. The entire battalion was brought together and housed in one camp, preparing for the latest Erskine initiative: first to remove the white farmers from their isolated homes, and then to create conditions for more traditional soldiering. There were plans for a 1,000-man sweep, supported by all arms. Somehow or other, led by intelligence never divulged to me, we were going to roll up the Mau Mau gangs operating out in the open. How these were to be identified was anybody's guess. Our role meanwhile was to drive about in Land-Rovers looking for trouble.

Some settlers refused to budge. After the First World War, land could be got on plains like these at a halfpenny an acre and the men who took up the offer were soon to be struck by economic collapse in the thirties. Perhaps at that time, Kenya was the least considered of colonies, a film location waiting to be discovered, with no story in it more appealing than the life of the white hunter. But postwar, trade had been booming and the country pushed into prominence as a British colony that worked, in the sense of turning a profit. No matter how the White Highlands had been acquired from the indigenous Kikuyu, no insurrection was going to queer the pitch. In moving from the forest to the plain, we had arrived at the real political cockpit of the Emergency – and, coincidentally, the common European perception of what the country looked like.

When I finally came home, many people asked me why I wasn't more tanned. Their understanding of Kenya was based on the 1953 film *Mogambo*, a vehicle for Clark Gable and Ava Gardner, shot in temperatures of 40 degrees Celsius. Miss Gardner's dismay at the dust and heat was further compounded by arguments with the film's director John Ford and the gloomy, irritable presence of her husband of a year, Frank Sinatra. (There's a quiz question here somewhere: what connects Frank Sinatra with Dedan Kimathi and General China?)

The move to the plains was one way of meeting the neighbours, the White Highlanders, their insufferable arrogance shaded by an additional and awful sadness, as if the life and the land that they were fighting to retain were nothing more than a nursing home for dull old actors. Hughie and his wife – the couple I had met on the train to Mombasa – were safely out of it, but many of their acquaintance were still in place.

We met them at cocktail parties thrown by the CO, to which they arrived already drunk, driving battered Peugeots and wandering into the mess toting pistols in cowboy holsters. Shorts added to the impression they gave of wizened schoolboys. Their ladies were dressed in cream linen skirt-suits from another era and they made fond enquiries about restaurants and nightclubs in London of which I had never heard.

'Well, have you ever seen the Lunts?' a balloon of a woman demanded, downing her fifth champagne cocktail.

'Are those in Cornwall?' a young man asked politely, thinking perhaps of rocks that were a danger to shipping.

As it happened I had seen Alfred Lunt and Lynn Fontanne (urged there by S) in a play that I forgot even in the act of leaving the theatre.

'She came originally from Woodford, you know.'

'Miss Fontaine?'

'I think we pronounce it Fontanne,' Mrs Watson said with great condescension. I noticed she was wearing grubby and unlaced tennis shoes on her feet.

'Gout,' she explained, shortly before being led outside for a breath of fresh air. Rummaging for a cigarette in her handbag she revealed the butt of a Webley .45.

'People say at home: Muriel, you can't possibly live like this. Well, sucks to them and their horrible little houses. And *you*,' she added, brushing away my proffered lighter, 'are a bit of a toad.'

On a reconnaissance patrol we met another ancient local, a Canadian who had fought at Vimy Ridge. Still very spry, he jumped out of his Land-Rover bearing a carry-case used to store mortar shells, from which he produced a bottle of whisky and six tumblers. It occurred to me to ask him the question that General Erskine had asked Wally Cooper: what did he make of the Governor-General?

'Now there's a man who couldn't pour piss out of a boot if the instructions were written on the sole,' he replied amiably. 'And you young fellows can take another lesson from meeting me. I don't give a fairy's fiddle about what's good for common humanity in this ever-changing modern world. How about that?'

'You think things have gone to the dogs, sir?'

'Don't know where they've gone and don't much care. One day you'll feel the same as me, crazy old coot. And that's a promise.'

All this while, his Kikuyu servant sat in the back of the vehicle with a Lee-Enfield rifle across his knees, silent and impassive. After a couple more drinks, the old Canadian stepped away from the bonnet of the Land-Rover to indicate that he must get on to where he was going. It would have been a work of moments for him to repack his whisky bottle and glasses himself. Without a word being said, the Kikuyu clambered from the vehicle and did it for him.

There is a tail to this story. In my second week at Cambridge, another time-expired subaltern and I fell into a bitter row about Kenya, which ended with after-hours fisticuffs in Senate House Passage. He had spent his National Service with the Royal Artillery in North Wales and had the advantage of seeing the Kenya Emergency through the prism of left-wing journalism, with which he had sustained his sanity and his sense of apartness from what he called the system. It seemed inconceivable to him that I had not recognised the evil that I had been doing by suppressing the legitimate claims of an indigenous people for the return of their land and self-government. By his lights, I should have known what was going on right there under my nose. At the very least, I should repudiate it now and stop describing my sixteen months in Kenya as exhilarating. It was the use of this particular word that had led us to blows. I was, he said, just another member of the imperial police and, as such, complicit in murder and tyranny.

'It's a stain you'll never be able to wash clean.'

I went to bed that night with a split lip and a lot to think about. What was at the back of this altercation was something very much to do with what Artie the Canadian had called the ever-changing modern world. Since landing at Nairobi, I had not read a single book, nor glanced at a newspaper. Like Artie, even more so like Muriel, I had not read and pondered *Lucky Jim* or *Lord of the Flies* and certainly not – oh, most certainly not – the obscurely published (in its first edition) *Lolita*. Like them, I had not seen Brando in *On the Waterfront* nor listened to the first broadcast of *Under Milk Wood*.

For me, of course, these were mere grains of sand in the hourglass. But for Art and Muriel the Kenya Emergency foretold something much more serious. Their personal histories were being obliterated in a landslide of the new, triggered by something not to be imagined even twenty years earlier. The Empire, as these two had known it, was in its death throes. Anthony Eden's appallingly misconceived adventure over Suez was yet to deliver the *coup de grâce* to the fallen giant but already present in Britain was an educated class that considered it owed its imperial past next to nothing. The age of deference, of one race to another and one class to its betters, was over. If I had come home from the wars an unthinking conscript, for the white settlers the case was even worse. No amount of individual goodness, no trait of charity or act of loving kindness could ever be enough in extenuation. They were pariahs. In Britain, as in Kenya, they had been Mau Mau-ed.

In the last month or so of my time in the colony I was posted as an instructor to a battle training school in Naivasha in the Rift Valley. The recruits were all members of the Kenya Regiment. The sergeant instructor with whom I worked was a Glorious Gloucester who had been captured by the Chinese at the Imjin River, four days of nightmare in April 1951.

'They had an entire division coming up the hill,' he explained drily, 'and we had a wind-up gramophone and a record of "Goodnight Irene", which we put on as a kind of last waltz. And did they see the funny side of it? They did not.'

He shared with me his incredulity at the sauntering arrangements we found at Naivasha. The recruits' barracks were little more than a fraternity dorm and great exception was taken at the idea of having them inspected, or even entered. Towels flew from the windows like prayer flags. Payday was a stroll to the office to collect a monthly cheque, made up of a civilian salary plus regimental pay.

Anything we might have to teach these recruits was received in more or less polite contempt.

'If I can hit a running buck at a hundred yards, man, I can sure as hell knock over some Kuke with his arse hanging out his trousers,' a blond giant advised me, adding with a knowing smirk, 'Christ, I've had enough practice.'

At weekends, the entire intake jumped into their cars and disappeared back to Nairobi, barely troubling the orderly room for passes. The Gloucester sergeant shrugged and sat by his crate of Tusker, smoking cheroots and telling me stories about his wife and her sister, his gran and – most fondly remembered of all – his children or, as he called them, anklebiters.

'I like their toys,' he mused. 'Little tanks, tiny little people and, same time, cows bigger'n houses. The girl has a dolly that closes her eyes when she wants to sleep. I like all that.'

'What about guns?'

'Oh, they got them too. All sorts. Has there ever been a better smell than a kid's toybox? I don't think so.'

'You spoil them,' I suggested. He smiled.

''S what they're for. What we're doing here, you and me, that's not life.'

'So what is?'

'Digging plasticine out the carpet with the bread-knife,' he suggested, passing me another Tusker. On his forearm, under a budding rose, was his wife's name, tattooed on flesh that had so narrowly avoided being turned to dust on the Imjin ridge.

As a farewell present to the indolent recruits, I took them

on a blistering hike around the perimeters of Lake Naivasha, circling in the process some hundreds of thousands of pink flamingos. We ran the whole way, toting packs and weapons. There was a hairdryer wind blowing soda dust into our eyes and choking our throats. The Gloucester sergeant declined the invitation to take part but two thirds of the way round, at the knee-buckling stage, we came across him. He had driven out from the camp in a Land-Rover, against which he was leaning nonchalantly, a bottle of beer dangling from two fingers. I don't know why, but as we stumbled past in our own little dust-devil, his sardonic smile and casually wafted salute have stayed with me as the perfect full stop to my time in National Service.

I had taken part in a small war and killed half a dozen fanatical men, of whose cause I knew next to nothing, in scenarios that no amount of Wordsworth could have prepared me for. I could do things and think things that I would never have the need to do or think again. But most important of all, I had let go some of the cumbersome baggage of childhood. While I was hardly a man, I was at any rate no longer a boy. All this, it seemed to me, was to be found in the Gloucester sergeant's laconic salute out by the lake, where the flamingos screeched and the perfectly flat landscape that we ran around seemed to heave like an ocean. I had seen a fraction of what this man had seen. What was a mere seven miles of choking dust to the images etched in his memory: the two VCs awarded that day, the ever-shrinking perimeters, the promise of death or mutilation on an otherwise utterly forget-table ridge? Sometimes the other ranks of the army – left to their own devices – get things exactly right and this flipped salute was the best of goodbyes. It was 'Goodnight Irene' all over again.

Chapter Six

THE WAY TO LOOK AT NATIONAL SERVICE, I DISCOV-
ered, was to see it as an interlude. For many people it was also
unwelcome servitude. My schoolboy friend, the Wrestler, had
spent two years in the RAF at High Wycombe, doing mind-
numbing clerking duties. The only interesting thing that
happened to him was when the equivalent of the office
manager, a squadron leader, had invited him back to his quar-
ters on the pretext of listening to a bit of Sibelius and opened
the door in a red suspender belt and bra. But even this was
high drama compared to the tales told of soldiers earning
their weekend pass by clipping the CO's lawn with nail scis-
sors or painting coal white. Some had spent two years sitting
at the back desks of orderly rooms in Berlin shuffling papers
on squaddies with pox or the exact number of gas capes held
in store but rated unserviceable.

By comparison I had a story to tell, though it turned out
to be unpopular. I was the sardine that had escaped the
canning factory.

*

The plane bringing me into London flew over a landscape of such staggering greenness that it caused a lump in my throat. The experience of looking down on bomb-bursts of leafy trees and the repeated rectangles of suburban lawns was far more awesome than touching down at Nairobi ever had been. It was like coming home to an altogether strange country, placid and somnolent in a bath of gently diffused sunlight. Occasional silver stabs from windscreens of cars breasting a hill, little miniatures of a cricket match or a village gymkhana: all these were novelties but they were not the story. That lay in the syncopated beauty of elms lining a river or an isolated oak in a field of stubble. Dazed by green, it was my patrimony that I was seeing through such disbelieving eyes.

The figures in the landscape revealed themselves in a similarly slant light. I thought that I knew what it was to be English but two boisterous years in the mob had dulled my senses. I came home to a country filled with people who still retained an essential shyness as their first response to strangers. The bluster and flimflam of army life, its cynicism and occasional brutality, were suddenly revealed as mere dialect. My countrymen spoke something different. On buses and trains, in cafés and pubs, the prevailing atmosphere was politely non-committal. Churchill had gone, Attlee was going, austerity was over. The patience and modesty that had tolerated pillboxes, tank-traps and all the rest of the wartime landscape were now a settled habit of mind.

I went back to Bury St Edmunds to hand in my kit.

Gibraltar Barracks too seemed a different place, much smaller than I remembered. In the quartermaster's stores, an elderly corporal set about reclaiming the army's property, down to drawers/cellular/green, pairs three. I confessed that I no longer had them. The corporal sucked his teeth. Could I at least provide the remnants, some scraps of linen, anything green that even remotely resembled a pair of drawers? Dust bounced in the sunlight as I tried to explain where I had come from.

'Otherwise, the cost'll be docked from your last pay, see?' the corporal persisted gently.

There was a courtesy interview with the commanding officer, who pressed me to sign on for another three years, an offer that he may have been charged to make by the War Office. When I declined, he edged around his desk and shook my hand, hoping, as he put it, that all the same we might meet again one day on the field of battle. I wondered for a moment whether he knew something I did not but the orderly room was reassuringly unprepared for conflict. A solitary clerk sat typing, hitting the keys one at a time, examining each impression with intense suspicion.

There was nobody else about and nothing to keep me. I walked into town lugging the cardboard suitcase that my mother had bought me at a jumble sale two years earlier. It had once been pale green, but mould and mud had reduced its colour to expressionistic camouflage. The strap tugged at its imitation-leather anchors. To get this case onto the plane at Nairobi within the weight limitations, I had opened it up and given away two pairs of handmade boots, a small mound of shirts and slacks and what few books I had scratted together. Even in the hollow spaces of an airport, these items gave off a pungent stink.

I set the case down on its home ground – a deserted Bury St Edmund's café – and ordered a cup of tea. Half an hour earlier I had been a gentleman, at least by the Queen's elastic definition of a subaltern. Now I was like a prisoner released from jail. The tenth of my life that I had given to the army was just so much smoke and ash. I was wearing the school blazer that I had bought three years earlier and had in my pocket a rail warrant and a fistful of coins, some of them as useless to me as plumber's washers.

There was no warning in this tea bar, with its ruined checked tablecloths and condensation running down the windows, of what was to befall when, twenty-five years later and quite by chance, I found myself back in the town on the way to somewhere else. For old times' sake, I tried to search out Gibraltar Barracks and asked directions of a man watering his lawn. He stared and then pointed downwards with his free hand. His house and those of his neighbours were built on the parade ground where Sergeant Holyoake had once taught me how to fix bayonets, advance in open order and present arms to the scudding and horizontal rain.

Waltham Cross was difficult. During my absence, my mother had moved on to soft furnishings as her emotional solace.

Where before she had bought jumble sale sweaters to unpick, now she sought out end-of-roll fabrics at what my old boss Mr Fishpool called 'monster giveaway prices'. It was the price that mattered more than the design or colour, leading to lime-green cushions arranged on orange loose covers and such. The wood lathe that was once hidden in the shed from prying eyes had clearly been busy and we had enough table lamps for a small brothel, each shaded by some shriekingly inappropriate bit of flash – purple, ivory, burnt sienna, gold. Upstairs, my bedroom was decorated with a thirties standard lamp bearing a massive shade that my mother had recovered in green and yellow stripes. The bedspread was Prussian blue.

My father's restless energy had led him to paper one wall of the dining room with red and blue poppies nearly two feet across, set off by a bamboo trellis design on the other three. Outside, the famous lawn glowed emerald. Sometime since I left, he had gone in for dahlias in a big way and was in the habit of going up to London on the commuter train like a bleeding funeral director, his arms filled with floral tributes. Neither of them asked a single question about Kenya: he out of spite, she because for all she knew Kenya was just across the Channel somewhere.

'How many letters did I get from you?' she demanded over a cup of tea. 'Six.'

'There was a war on.'

'All the more reason to keep in touch. Your father's joined

the Civil Defence. When they drop the bomb, which'll be any day now, everyone's got to piss on their sheets and hang them up at the window. They give you four minutes to do that. Then you wait three weeks, or is it three months? Anyway, the headquarters is at Cheshunt Library and your father's in charge, so we're in safe hands.'

'He's in charge?'

She smiled.

'When you went away, you forgot your dinner jacket. I gave it a bit of a sponge last weekend, cos I suppose you'll be gadding about a bit from now on.'

'Not in that,' I promised.

'Do they let you home at all? Someone was telling me it lasts three years, this college stuff.'

'The terms are only eight weeks long.'

'Your kind of job, then.'

She had begun serious cooking, using it as a means to challenge my father when he rolled in from the commuter train. The portions were huge, a thing he hardly seemed to notice. Most meals concluded with an apple pie, of which he ate exactly half, maybe with a bit of Cheddar on the side. It seemed to me, who had temporarily forgotten much of the war between Bert and Peggy, that she was trying to murder him with carbohydrates. He ate until he was blue in the face and then tottered out to his garden, in these autumn months inspecting it by the light from the lean-to, a blank and tubby figure wafting a Gold Flake. Alf next door told me that in high summer Bert rose at dawn for a little light hoeing and weeding before setting off to work.

Neil was the most welcoming. He had shot up in height and had been picked for the primary school football team, a lanky kid with knobbly knees and God-given ball sense. My father, as had been foretold when his second son was a mere baby, found him wanting in the same way that I had been but for different reasons. Neil's good nature and – unusual in our house – complete lack of petulance surprised and irritated Bert: he thought him lazy.

'What sort of animals did you see out there?' my brother asked, chin in hands at the dining-room table, fair hair flopping.

I told him how I had tried to get Abbassi a medal of some kind for killing a rhino that had gored a soldier. The rhino had arrived in a tearing hurry, knocked his victim down and then, horrifically, began rolling on him. Abbassi (ever a man of few words) strolled over and, kneeling on a ton of enraged grey and mauve beast, pulled back its ear and emptied an entire magazine of Sten into its brain.

'Poor old rhino.'

'Brave soldier.'

'Yeah,' Neil muttered, uncertain.

Round at George and Vi's there was an atmosphere. S, as she was well entitled to do, had been seeing someone else. It was perhaps more accurate to say that she had been laid siege to by a co-worker at the bank. Roy was exactly what I would have become without the aggressive interventions of Hertford Grammar School: moony, sentimental to a fault, star-struck. The previous Christmas, when I was being carried out of the bamboo in delirium, he had shocked Vi to her roots by turning up, unannounced, at the annual wingding of senior members of the family in Cheshunt. Tall, gangling and nine years older than S, he conducted an antiquated form of courtship. What he had to offer her he elaborated in a faintly lugubrious and self-slaughtering way. He was William Guppy pursuing Esther Summerson in *Bleak House*.

But then, who was I? Smoking a pipe with a circle of sopping-wet black soldiers in the depths of the Aberdares was one thing. Smoking it while walking back to the Cross from S's was twice as dangerous. Who was this drip in desert boots and flimsy cotton kecks who dared to poke his nose in where honest men drank? In the saloon bar of the Gun and Magpie they talked allotments and football. I knew little of either and was new to pub culture, ordering as my first civilian drink in Britain a pint of stout and mild, which was seen by the locals as a gross, possibly foreign, perversion. When I followed that up with a blushing request for a brandy and ginger, the jig was up.

'Then what?' a large man demanded. ''Ow about a gin and vermoof?'

He got his laugh. He and his mates had me pegged, not just as a stranger to their pub but alien in a way they did not like. I sat alone at a table, flipping up place mats with the bitter realisation that all the banter with Wally Cooper had been based on a deception. He had indulged me during our time together because he had no choice in the matter. The Gun and Magpie would have found *him* odd – too loquacious, too much of a balding fat boy – but tolerable. A twenty-year-old kid who smoked a pipe and only ordered drinks if they were mixed with other drinks was either weak in the head or taking the piss.

There was another reason for their show of disdain. I had come out of the army with the tic of excessively polite address, something I associated with the manners that makyth subalterns. I had lost the knack of saying what I thought.

'Come on, spit it out,' my father more than once badgered, impatient with this or that anecdote of life in the Aberdares.

In Kenya, a mannered way of talking had gone unnoticed, but in places like the Gun and Magpie it marked me out. I, who had so recently blown other human beings to kingdom come, was, in the England to which I had returned, a bit of a weed. So far as saloon bars went, I managed to combine two dangerous failings: to be unthreatening but at the same time conspicuous.

'You don't half speak posh,' my mother said. The idea alarmed me. 'I'm not complaining,' she added. 'Though wouldn't it be a bloody laugh if it was you that turned out to be the nob in the family?'

'The nob?'

'Yes. For example, have you ever thought of being a dentist? They earn a screw to make your eyes water. Go on, ring them up at this college and say you want to be a dentist.'

'I could wear my dinner jacket to the Dentists' Ball, eh?'

'You've really got it in for that tux, haven't you? That cost me thirty shillings, I'd have you know.'

'Well,' said Vi loyally, 'they must have some nice shops out there because you've come back with a very smart sports jacket, I'll say that.'

It, and a few souvenir carvings, were the only things I came back with that I had not owned when I set out. I explained how I had been sent by the president of the mess one afternoon to buy fresh stocks of whisky and gin at an Asian store in Nyeri. On the face of it, nothing could have been simpler. But the Aziz family, father and son, saw me coming. Flattered, teased, given mint tea for the stomach, pressed to sample shortbread biscuits baked in the Queen's beloved Highlands, I was led gently into a conversational maze, only narrowly avoiding being sold a radiogram in a walnut-finish cabinet.

'I am living in a *tent*,' I yelped.

'If you don't want, sell to someone else and that way make good business,' the younger Aziz suggested.

After two hours of chiding and beseechment I walked out with a case of whisky and the jacket. At some point in the afternoon, I had incautiously agreed to try it on, causing Aziz Senior to clap his hands in a mixture of astonishment and pleasure. However many times I tried to take it off again, he begged me to give him the continued joy of seeing it modelled the way that the tailor had intended.

'Well,' I capitulated weakly, 'how much is it, then?'

'About such a garment, we are not mentioning money,' Mr Aziz reproved. He seized my hands in his. 'You are English gentleman and surely-to-goodness a gentleman demands only the best? I think so. That has been made always very clear to me, ever since I was young boy.'

George laughed at the story but Vi was confused. In her eyes, I had come home a spoiled print, much as you get when two images are exposed on the same frame of film. I had left a boy and now here I was back again as some sort of half-baked sophisticate with a line in bazaar stories. Who knew or cared what it was like in Africa? The burning question was: what was I going to do about Roy? She never voiced these anxieties but you could see they were there at the back of her mind.

Two years had much altered S. At the bank, young though she was, she was already earmarked for higher things. Her faintly emphatic way of speaking, the colossal fund of common sense she possessed and perhaps, most of all, her loyalty to the institution made her a clerk with huge added value. She dressed for the role, managing to look both chaste and stylish, a girl with a purpose in life. Right at the edge of her peripheral vision, like a knifeblade of light at the sea's horizon, was something so obvious that only a fool like me could miss it: a determination to get out of Enfield Lock, its allotments and church socials, snobby tennis clubs and Sunday football leagues, at all costs.

About Roy, she was calm itself.

'It's not as if you and I are engaged or anything,' she pointed out. 'And I don't suppose you were living like a monk yourself. In fact, I don't know what you were doing. You're not a great letter-writer, are you?'

'Oh, is that the attraction with Roy?'

'Roy's a lot of fun. Or he can be.'

'Clever girl,' my father commented. 'I see her on the train occasionally. Too good for you, chum. *She* could have gone to university. But what did she do? She knuckled down and got on with it.'

He spoke as he always did about Cambridge, right to the very end. Going to university was the postponement of something far more serious, something he liked to describe as the real world. The place he had in mind ran on money and power over others. Its operations were brutal but had the advantage of rendering shape from chaos. You knew where you were in the real world.

In searching for a way to describe my father's pleasure in this concept, I am reminded of visiting Margam steelworks in the days of its pomp. I was watching one of the furnaces belch flame and sparks as men in aprons flung a shovel of this or that into the crucible, when I felt a colossal scorching heat, enough to add the smell of burning wool from my jacket to the tart, almost vinegary air. I looked around, and approaching on the rails that I was standing on was a white-hot container bearing molten steel. It was nobody's job but mine to step out of the way and avoid being crisped. The man who was guiding me around the plant continued explaining things in a perfectly unemotional and conversational way. He had not even noticed the moment take place.

It was the sort of venue that would have filled Bert with delight – one mistake and you're done for. In his view of things, Cambridge and its raving poofs would have changed the molten steel into something less threatening, like marshmallows, or a *vendange* of Muscadet grapes. He had no power of wit in him and his scorn was unmediated and – I would like to think – abysmally ignorant. But enrolling S into his world-view was alarming. Once or twice, I caught myself looking at her with an outsider's eye.

'You're not making too much of a meal about this Roy thing, are you?' she asked.

'You were right. We're not engaged or anything.'

'What a horrible thing to say.'

'I'm only repeating what *you* told *me*,' I protested.

'You've come home a very changed person. Everyone's noticed it.'

'Everyone? Who's everyone?'

'Oh, you're so full of yourself. So conceited. Well, I should go off to university if I were you. I'm sure you'll fit in very well.'

In the movies, from which I derived much of my emotional language, I could turn on my heel and walk away down the rainswept pavements; or she could put on a cute little hat and white gloves and catch the train out of the city, her face at the window mingling with reflections of the life from which she was fleeing. At some point Cary Grant would engage her in conversation.

Instead, we stood outside the Enfield Highway Co-op trying to outstare each other. When she turned and walked the hundred yards or so to her house alone, it was drama enough.

Going back to Cambridge as an undergraduate was an odd experience. In the neighbourhood where I had lived as a child the university had been tolerated but by no means loved. Very few townies could identify more than one or two colleges by name and even when they directed strangers to the 'Christ's bus-stop' or 'the post office opposite Trinity', they were indicating general and unspecific landmarks, as a cowpoke might direct the city dude to the cow and calf rock or three lone pines. As for students, Town Cambridge knew nothing of them other than their capacity to clutter up the pavements, ruin pubs with their braying and swell the queues for cinemas.

I am struck today by how much students are perceived – and see themselves – as a subset of a general youth culture. Dousing your chum with baked beans or shaving foam at the conclusion of his finals would have seemed extraordinarily infantile then, just as women students with tattoos or braided hair would have announced themselves as pathetic exhibitionists. The business of undergraduates was to stand aloof from the common culture, an apartness heartily encouraged by the town.

'William is well on his way to a double first,' someone cried in my time there, his voice filling the pub as if the locals were just so much furniture. 'What he doesn't know about Feuerbach isn't worth knowing, really. His mind is shimmeringly awesome.'

'But he can't fuck for toffee,' the barmaid Rosie muttered, convulsing the regulars gathered around the dartboard.

In my first year at Trinity I lived out of college in circumstances not much different to life in the Cross. On my first day in student digs Mrs Wilson showed me upstairs to a back bedroom, going out of her way to tell the story of a young gentleman who had arrived drunk the previous evening, climbed onto a desk, opened the window with too much of a flourish and tumbled head over heels into Mr Wilson's shed. The hole in the roof was plain to see. He had, she said with great satisfaction, been taken away by ambulance and would probably never walk again.

'That won't happen to me,' I said.

'No, it won't. Because I shall see to it that it doesn't.'

Mrs Wilson ran Mr Wilson ragged in her part of the house and saw no reason to change her tune with me. The accommodation she offered was curiously old-fashioned, a sort of Noël Coward image of how the respectable poor lived. I looked around me in mild despair. A single bed bearing a faded grey-green eiderdown lurked against one wall. There was a scuffed and battered Rexine armchair, a desk and a cupboard cabinet. On the wall was a Corot print scissored from some magazine and stuffed behind glass in a flyblown mount. A small wardrobe completed the inventory. In an attempt to show my appreciation I tugged on its door and the whole thing tipped forward like a willing drunk. There was a strained silence.

'The man downstairs is foreign,' Mrs Wilson said before leaving, her eyes glittering.

Danek Bienkowski was reading Natural Sciences. He was an amiable young Pole who had come to Cambridge to peer into the deeper recesses of matter, play tennis (which he did to a very high standard) and meet interesting girls. In his wallet he kept a record of the films he had seen, marked out of ten – and, more combustibly, a newspaper clipping from the *Daily Mail*, claiming that Polish men made irresistible lovers. Shortly after our arrival, he showed this item to a girl he met in the Rex Cinema and brought her back to Mrs Wilson's. This vile woman immediately sent her husband out into the garden to spy on them under the pretence of clipping the hedge. Standing on the topmost rung of a stepladder, peering over the transom of the french windows, the luckless Wilson was so taken by what he saw that he overtoppled and crashed to the ground, gashing the bridge of his nose and scuffing both elbows.

'What did he see?' I asked Danek.

'We were talking about Kim Novak,' he said. 'In *Pffft*. I give it eight out of ten, by the way. These bloody people are mad. You can imagine what happened. Wendy did a bunk through the front door and won't ever talk to me again.'

I had my own disappointments in that line. Figgie had married an RAF technician. I found this out at the Cambridge Jazz Club and for a moment the whole dance hall reeled. The girl who told me patted my arm. She asked whether I wanted Figgie to know I was back. I said no.

'You're probably right.'

'Are they happy?'

'She married him, didn't she?' She considered for a moment. 'One thing's for sure, she'd throw a blue fit if she knew you were back in Cambridge.'

Two nights later, I cycled into Hall for dinner, jumped off my bike and, stuffing my pipe into Mr Aziz's jacket, slotted in at the last refectory table. A servant ladled me some very thin potato soup.

'God, it stinks in here,' my neighbour grumbled.

'Something on the hot plates, maybe.'

It was uncomfortably warm and I opened my jacket to get some air.

A gout of flame leaped out. The same servant was passing with a jug of water.

'Excuse me, sir,' he said, 'I do believe you're on fire.'

So saying, he tossed the contents of the jug over my chest with a deft hand.

'Extraordinary!' my neighbour exclaimed. 'Was it a cigarette or something?'

'An old love letter.'

On the top table, this little conflagration had caught the attention of the Master of Trinity, Lord Adrian. He paused, a spoonful of soup halfway to his lips. For a brief moment, our eyes locked.

The supervisor of my studies was Helena Shires, whose husband Teddy had devised the numbering and dismantlement of the stained glass in King's College Chapel at the outbreak of war. Mrs Shires was warm and even merry at our weekly meetings. My predecessor on her treacherously capacious couch had been the recently graduated poet Thom Gunn; I always thought of her as having shifted down several gears when it came to teaching me. My prose style delighted her for its defects, not least of which was the search for a main verb.

'Really,' she said with great good humour, 'you should look to say what you mean and not try to please me with such wonderful elaborations of what you might mean, given a bit of a nudge in the right direction. And hang the critics, incidentally. I want to be able to say of you, "Oh, *oh*, this is what he thinks of Skelton." You may take it for granted that I know what *I* think. Surprise me, therefore. Confound me!'

We drank coffee and nibbled at cake while the phone rang and dogs barked in her architect-designed thirties house. A Swedish au pair of stunning beauty moved about from room to room, replacing books on shelves and gathering up papers and journals, only very occasionally meeting my hungry glance. I always walked out of these supervisions lightheaded, mooching along back to the centre of Cambridge in a mixture of elevation and despair. I was dressed in what amounted to the first-year uniform: corduroy jacket and cavalry twill trousers, over which was a duffle coat of faintly North African provenance, not at all the stuff of Arctic convoys and destroyer bridges, more suited to the selling of oranges.

I was having image problems generally. The umbrella that I bought from Woolworth's was hardly a week old when the handle parted from the business end and – I was swishing it nonchalantly at the time – the spokes and fabric flew off and landed on the roof of a car that bore it away around the corner. An almost identical misfortune happened a day or so later. Meeting the awesome Dr Redpath in Trinity Street and falling in with him the better to discuss balladry in a learned but bantering way, I flicked my pipe to clear it of dottle. The stem shot clear and posted itself down a road drain, leaving me with the lighted bowl in my fist. Redpath continued walking as though nothing at all had happened, save for one momentary twitch of his eyebrows.

'I am going into Heffer's,' he said gravely, making me a nod. At the door to the bookshop, a realisation burst upon him.

'Of course! You are the man who wrote to the college on NAAFI notepaper. I see who you are now.'

I cut around the corner and hid in the Rose, blushing and heavy with stupidity.

The first time that I walked into the faculty library, I sat down at a spare table that happened to have on it *Christopher Marlowe: Overreacher* by Harry Levin, a study of the play-wright based on the gloriously simple proposition contained in the title. I read it from cover to cover like a novel and then made my way to the Volunteer in Green Street in great good spirits. If this was the kind of critical stance required, then I would do well. The only practical obligation I had as a student was to turn up at Helena Shires's house once a week and read an essay to her. I could (and did) dispense with lectures to spend the balance of my time reading, smoking, and drinking the modified antifreeze that was Yugoslav Riesling, a chemically enhanced rotgut that stood just this side of blindness. I need not eat – possibly a sandwich or a cheese roll at lunchtime. At night I would stalk about in an undergraduate gown, gaunt and interesting to passers-by, but aloof. By these stratagems I would somehow or other acquire wisdom or, if not that, a fitful understanding of how difficult scholarship was.

There were problems even with this scheme of self-education, the chief being a very sketchy grasp of historical perspective. What I knew (for example) of the life lived by the majority of people in the fourteenth century – their hopes and fears, their secret disappointments and guilty pleasures – would not fill a page of any essay presented to Mrs Shires. The shorthand answer was of course provided by a single word: Chaucer. But was that enough? I spent a good deal of those early weeks with a toothglass full of Riesling, looking at the reflection of myself suspended above Mr Wilson's ruined shed and feeling trapped, trapped.

There was a branch of the London Soup Kitchen in Petty Cury and I fell into the habit of going there most mid-mornings. Black walls, bare floors and cappuccinos drunk from transparent cups gave it a louche atmosphere that seemed to be of particular attraction to former grammar-school boys. I think there was a reason for this. We had been raised in the dark, like rhubarb, with the promise that, once we were at university, the shed doors would be flung open and we would be seen for who we were in all our red and leafy glory. We had not realised – I had not realised – that the predominant tone set in most colleges was still that of the public school.

There happened to be a man at Trinity whom I knew slightly from army days. Sent to the Okehampton course to be toughened up by route marches and yomps over the moors, we were running up the hill to the camp in the last stages of exhaustion one morning when we were passed by this enterprising and Pickwickian figure in a cab that he had hired, his rifle, pack and helmet on the seat beside him. Now here we were again: I at Mrs Wilson's, he in a set of rooms in

Great Court. We talked one day outside the porters' lodge about reading and books.

'I know exactly what you mean,' he supplied generously to some maundering remark of mine. 'If I borrow a book from my father's library and omit to leave a slip in its place on the shelves, there really is the most fearsome row.'

He was not scoring a cheap point, but neither was it a conversation about books and libraries. He came from some other tradition, of wealth and privilege, of which I had known nothing until I came to Cambridge. I was Rhubarb Man; he some more rare and exotic plant.

My childhood chum the Wrestler (we had been to the same Cambridge grammar school) was an habitué of the soup kitchen, as was Danek. John 'Hoppy' Hopkins, surely the least likely physicist ever to be admitted to an undergraduate course, played vehement stride piano there. He had yet to become a jazz and rock photographer and friend of the Beatles, something that only came about when a doting relative gave him a single-lens reflex camera as a graduation present.

Another refugee from honest study was Rough Rog Tuckwell, a graduate student from Trinity who was to Australian Rules football what Danek was to Junior Wimbledon tennis. Like him, he carried a selection of press cuttings in his wallet, most of them lamenting the loss to Rules when Rough Rog gave up the pigskin for the pen. He had come 14,000 miles to research the likely effect of the newly ratified Treaty of European Union on the Australian wool trade. There was none, leaving him relieved and crest-fallen in about equal measure.

'I never even heard of bloody Chaucer, mate,' Rog said of my recited woes. 'Anyway, aren't all you blokes doing English only here for the shirt-lifting?'

One night we were drinking in the Still and Sugar Loaf, a pub he liked because it was sited underground and had some of the affect of his native Sydney. When it came time to leave, Rog knotted his BA gown around his waist and picked up a white enamel weighing machine which he carried out into the street. We had not gone very far before being stopped by two Bulldogs in their top hats. Rog stood hugging the weighing machine as the Proctor hove into view. He nodded with the utmost civility and raised his mortarboard.

'Good evening, sir. Leaving the weighing machine to one side for a moment, that is a very inappropriate way to wear a BA gown.'

'Yes,' Rog allowed. 'You got me there. But then that's a bloody silly hat you've got on your head, mate.'

Chapter Seven

FARCE AND UNCERTAINTY ON ONE FRONT; THE balancing of accounts on another. I came home at the end of the Michaelmas term to a more realistic appraisal of where I stood at Eastfield Road. Over the last eight weeks, my father had been brooding on the matter.

'Three more years of this and he'll end up in the nuthouse,' my mother explained. 'I mean, look at you.'

She was referring to the pipe that had destroyed my Nyeri jacket, a bright yellow calabash that passed (or so I supposed) without comment in Trinity Street but looked effete beyond words in Waltham Cross. As did the foulard scarf, the crew-neck beige sweater and cavalry twill trousers. There was no one in the Cross even remotely dressed like me, unless it was an amateur actor walking on for the Co-op Players as Gerald, the hapless and self-deluded novelist and poet, younger brother to Cynthia, Lady Bassingbourne, of Barmcake Hall, etc, etc. Peggy shook her head in despair.

'You know where Woolies is in Cambridge, don't you?

Couldn't you have gone in there and bought yourself a comb for Christmas?'

The dispute with my father went further than the question of how I dressed. I was at university on a means-tested county scholarship that made him an unwilling contributor to the costs of my education. It was this more than anything else that shifted our view of each other into its final form, one that lasted until his death. He owed me nothing as his son, and the debt – the one that mattered most because of the way the real world keeps its books – was all on the other side. Was I or was I not taking money from his pocket to waft about in an undergraduate gown on studies that left more than half the year free for what he called holidays? Was it his job to keep me in tobacco and beer the while? (It was easier to rebut his other charge, which was this: knowing that I was going to university, why had I not saved my army pay to help defray the expense?)

I tried to meet his points. Everybody should contribute to the personal costs of their university career and there was no dissent between us here. I had sufficient of my mother's hysteria about the imminent arrival of the broker's men not to get into debt during term time and I expected to pay my way for living at home the rest of the year. But that was not the nub of the matter.

I was the first in the family to go to university, though my cousin soon followed and completely outshone me, ending a distinguished academic career as Professor of Analytical

Chemistry at Birkbeck. But then Michael had Uncle Jim as a father, who, though he worked all his life as a car mechanic, had far more size about him than Bert. When Michael entered Imperial College as an undergraduate, it was a cause of celebration; he had taken on the best and triumphed. What everybody always knew about him – that he was a colossal brainbox – was vindicated by public examination. All that Jim asked of his son was that he did not come home as a tweedy member of the Drones Club, ending all his sentences with 'don'cha know' and smoking cigarettes through an amber holder.

I want to be fair to my own father, as much as is possible. He was an extremely intelligent man, driven by personal and sexual disappointments as wounding as any felt by his crazy wife. He could think and – when the occasion demanded – out-think others whose passage through life had been far smoother than his own. His reputation in the world of telecommunications was unimpeachable.

What he could not do was trust. He had great reason to feel this way but it blighted what was otherwise a glittering career. I had spent ten years of my life looking after a very erratic and bipolar mum while he was away in the RAF and for the time after the war when he came home, only for him to abandon us and live with his parents. 'Keeping Mum' was the phrase for it – and, much more to the point, keeping mum about what had gone on in his absence. My mother had cuckolded him with a number of more-or-less innocent

Americans and it did not make the story any sweeter that they, like him, were aircrew. This was the real stumbling block between us as men; even as a child I had somehow colluded in my mother's betrayal of him. Seen in this stark light, my place at Cambridge was an unjustified reward.

For nine vacations I worked at jobs he found me and at the end of each week surrendered to him my unopened wage packet. He gave me back spending money. The crowded envelope of banknotes he shoved so carelessly into his back pocket was not for my share of the cost of sausage and chips or shepherd's pie, and certainly none of it was heading my mother's way as cook and general skivvy. Taking money that he did not need enshrined his honestly held opinion of university education as a shameless contribution to the history of malingering. He had not needed a higher education. Why should he spend a penny of his own on mine?

'But going to university is a bit like work, isn't it?'

'What, with twenty-eight-week holidays?' he scoffed. 'Your idea of a good job, I don't doubt.'

'Would it make a difference if I was reading telephone engineering?'

'I'm not arguing with you. If you don't like it, you can clear off and make your own way. Get yourself a bedsit somewhere.'

'And how would I pay for it in term time?'

'Get yourself a weekend job. Do what others do.'

'Well, he has got a point,' Peggy mumbled. 'I'll give him

this: he don't owe nobody nothing for what he's made of himself.'

I was amazed to hear her say it, for in my eyes he had made himself a monster. She shrugged her bony shoulders and lit another cigarette. After a bit she shuffled out to chuck another shovel of coke into the Ideal boiler. I sat with my chin in my hands, bathed in the light of sudden understanding.

It was very simple. My father had it in for me whichever way I turned. To this day, whether he loved me or not I cannot say. But what was clear was that he did not like me far beyond what was normal in a parent of ordinary sensibilities. (Who was to say I was likeable, after all?) These feelings of his came from the gut. He did not like me the way he could not stand dogs or garden slugs.

All of which left me with the question: what was I going to do about it? In an image that comes easily from those times, I stopped staring at the wire and began digging the tunnel.

The first vacation job I had under my father's scheme began the very next day. Passing through Liverpool Street on his way to work, he signed me up as a relief railway porter. It was certainly a long way from Trinity Great Hall but not as character-forming as he might have wished. Moreover, it had consequences neither of us could have foretold.

You could describe railway portering of the period as money for Old Holborn. It was unskilled labour in all but one regard: there was a knack in dropping a promising-looking box just hauled from the goods van at exactly the right height onto its most vulnerable corner. When it was done properly, the packaging shattered and the contents were revealed. The rest was sleight of hand. The first time I saw this done, I had to blink twice to believe it, the more so because it was effected under the nose of a foreman porter there on purpose to prevent it. The theft that followed was accomplished as smoothly and routinely as a laundress folding sheets.

We took our breaks in an underground mess at the end of one of the platforms, an unheated hell-hole littered with the crusts of sandwiches, newspapers and cigarette packets. Rats ran around the walls the way they do in pantomime sketches, as if drawn on strings; nobody seemed to notice. Some had come to work only to sleep, others to add to an open-ended seminar on horse-racing that had probably begun the day the station opened in 1874. The place reeked of soot and sulphur, as did the whole station, while above ground there was always an additional mysterious stink, as if from a nearby fish quay.

Though the job was massively overmanned, we porters remained largely invisible to the travelling public, even when pushing truckloads of the Christmas cards they had written or were destined to receive. We mooched about in the permanent twilight to be found under the canopy, sometimes wielding a broom for a few minutes to show willing but disappearing at the first sign of a passenger with a luggage problem.

A seasoned porter called Chas took me on as his assistant and for half the ten-hour shift we would walk, a couple of buckets of sand in each hand, up some stairs and across a creaking cast-iron gantry before leaving them in a corner while we nipped into Bishopsgate for a wet. Then we would stagger back with them to our underground cave for a smoke. The only time anything like despatch was shown was the day the royal family set off for Sandringham. On that morning half the station staff mobbed the train, hustling for the honour of lifting a suitcase into the compartments assigned to the entourage. The knack here was to avoid the equerries, who had seen a thing or two before joining the Palace, and go for elderly ladies-in-waiting, who responded with bewildered gratuities.

'I'm afraid I don't have any coin in my purse,' one said.

'Don't you worry about that, ma. Me and my family wish you and yours a very Merry Christmas.'

Blushing, she passed across a green pound note.

Chas was thin and wiry, with a boxer's broken nose. If he ever washed or changed his shirt and underwear, it was not in the winter months. He reeked. His was a soon-told story. He had not meant to stay long in the job, which he took up in the year and month that I was born. As he said, he could not for the life of him explain why he was still there. On Wednesdays we did the pools together. I asked him about his family.

'Just the usual,' he said absently.

The travelling public were almost as invisible to us as we were to them, though Chas liked to lean against the platform barrier when the evening rush hour started because he had a dark theory about brassieres. In the old days even a duchess would stuff what she'd got into a couple of bags and leave it at that. But nowadays you'd see kiddies, even well-set-up women, walking onto Nine and Ten – the commuter platforms we serviced – with what looked like ice-cream cones stuck up their jumpers.

'It's to do with America,' he explained. '*Their* bloody women have to look like guns. You know, them ray-guns.'

Chas showed sublime indifference to how things wagged at Cambridge, fifty miles down the line. If he thought about it at all, I believe he would have taken it for granted that educated people had their own arrangements to make that did not include him. Habit had made him a drudge, but an uncomplaining one. He worked overtime if he could get it, and when he could not, waved me a weary goodbye as he sloped off up the concourse to have one before going home.

He was the perfect antidote to romantic idealism about the unawakened working class. Unawakened he certainly was. I had never met anyone with such an economy of speech and gesture. Even drinking with him was done in silence. Though he was on nodding terms with the landlord he never addressed him nor anyone else in the pub by name. We took our seats on a ruined red plush bench and sat side by side like companionable mutes. Most of the time Chas stared at the shape his hand made on the table, or the browny collar on the glass of Mann's. Occasionally he would wipe his nose on his sleeve.

'I met a bloke in the army who cleaned the vats for that lot,' I offered once.

'What lot?'

'Mann's.'

He nodded, as though acknowledging a child's harmless prattle.

I used to fantasise about taking Chas to meet my tutor Helena Shires. She would have treated him with the respect she showed everybody in life but his suffocated quietism might have baffled her. He fell beneath the threshold of literature – even the endlessly curious Chaucer would have passed him over without a second glance. He was like an uncomplaining dog, who knew the station, the pub across the road and the short walk home – but nothing more. One day his joints would stiffen or his colon gripe and that would be the end of him. Prod as I might, I could not get a single opinion out of him. Was Christmas a special time of year? He shrugged.

'Boxing Day we go round Harry's,' he mumbled.

One evening, we were leaning on our brooms and studying the chests of typists staggering home from office parties, when a gaunt and faintly theatrical figure loomed out of the roiling gloom. It was Roy. I swept around his feet with a few passes.

'You know why I'm here,' he said for openers.

'If not, you're going to tell me.'

He turned to Chas.

'Can I borrow your mate for a minute or two?'

We walked to the end of the platform, where the soot and grit met gusts of watery and disappointing London snow. The tracks glistened silver before disappearing under boxlike tunnels. We were in a film moment.

'S told me where to find you. I thought of coming down to Cambridge and seeing you there but it wouldn't have been the right thing.'

'How is S?'

'You know very well how she is, you rat! I love that woman. We have so many things in common. We're both Londoners for a start.'

'*I'm* a bloody Londoner,' I said, outraged.

'I don't think so,' Roy smiled, shaking his head sorrowfully. 'I mean you might be now, but university is going to change all that, isn't it? I don't see you walking down this platform for the rest of your life. But I will.'

We stood staring into inky shadows. I could feel something shifting inside me. I had only to say 'She's yours' for Christmas to take on a new character for all three of us. Not just Christmas either: the rest of our lives. Roy peered at me hopefully as if trying to read my mind.

'You're a bit late going home tonight, aren't you?' I temporised.

'You think I've been in the pubs. That's not my way. I've been walking.'

'Whereabouts?'

'What does it matter whereabouts?' he shouted, loud enough to make me jump. 'I want you to give her up. You're not right for her but I can make her happy.'

I noticed for the first time that he was wearing gloves and for some reason this turned me against him. It was completely irrational – why not wear gloves in cold weather? – but it pricked an irritation in me that I had not felt until then.

'Get stuffed, Roy.'

He jerked back as if slapped. All this while Chas was watching, sitting on a barrow and rolling a matchstick-thin cig. Roy walked back towards him, beating at his temples with his fancy gloves.

'What if I threw myself under a train?' he yelled at me over his shoulder.

'Not off this platform you won't, mate,' Chas said.

Instead, he wandered away to a little symphony of door slams, whistles, sudden sharp cries, escaping steam and, floating over all, station announcements that were so over-amplified to be utterly unintelligible. '*Na-argh... poofacker... orcat weasel... chemni billyar, Goglung, chabberklink an chew.*'

And then: '*Kerchkk... Chkk!*' followed by the strains of 'We Wish You a Merry Christmas', sung by a children's choir.

And that was it: Roy was toast. S and I set about three years of renewed courtship. Our needs had come together like locking pieces of a jigsaw. She wanted to make something of herself in an environment more promising than Enfield Lock and I had to find the big Elsewhere that I would need to prosper in as my own man. These were not cloudy ambitions but imperatives. We were partners, therefore, and the commonest way of expressing this was to say we were in love.

A text was to hand. It was 1955, the year of *Love is a Many Splendored Thing*, perhaps the postwar cinema's greatest weepie to date, in which William Holden and Jennifer Jones reduced audiences to emotional pulp with the story of a doomed – doubly doomed – love affair. The film was directed by the sixty-nine-year-old veteran cynic Henry King, who five years earlier had entranced me with the all-male war movie *Twelve O'Clock High*. On that occasion I left the Regal in Cambridge as a tragic B-17 pilot, only to be shot down all over again by my first encounter with the sardonic and glamorous Figgie, the teenager from heaven.

I saw the later film with S at the Embassy in Waltham Cross, in company with a couple of hundred other romantics. It was the time when people queued to get into cinemas and I think we did that too, settling at last into an auditorium that smelled of wet coats, dank hair and cough sweets. It soon became clear that this was a story about the heart ambushed by circumstance. Little by little as the story unfolded, the girls in the audience gave way to quiet sobbing. When it was all over (as signalled by a heavenly choir) we came out onto the rainy misery of the Cross in a half-laughing, half-crying crowd. We had been manipulated by experts.

The book and film are based on a very brief adulterous affair that the writer Han Suyin (played on the screen by Jennifer Jones) had with a married *Times* reporter killed in Korea in 1952. Miss Suyin was in her thirties when she wrote this work. But S and I were only twenty and had no clear idea of what we meant by love, many-splendoured or otherwise. The obvious explanation was that we meant different things, or different things at different times. Looking back, I am amazed that this did not trouble us more.

The ideal of existence for us both was not Hong Kong, where *Love is a Many Splendored Thing* was set, but a cottage with roses over the door, work we liked to do and time to spend the money we earned. A village would be too constricting but a small market town might fit the bill. (I cannot drive through Tetbury in Gloucestershire without thinking of the sort of thing we had in mind. In fact, I have spent half a century looking for the place we *might* have found, expressed as bricks and mortar.) The dream life would include books, to be sure, but also period furniture, transfer-ware bowls and dishes, French wines and garden rollers. I would play cricket, which I had never done in my life. S would astonish the neighbours with her profiteroles and business acumen. Our children would walk about under the apple trees and confide their thoughts to squirrels.

Had we met even ten years later, in the sixties, the awful redundancy of these ideas would have been exposed and things might have taken a very different turn. More tellingly still, were S and I to meet for the first time today, the day you are reading this page, magically rewound to our early thirties, not one of the things that we thought then would now be of the slightest use to us. What we talked about so earnestly on our tramps through Enfield or on the last train home from Liverpool Street would not even cross our minds. Owlish, immature, yet willing ourselves into middle age, we were two innocents – and, for all our bookish aspirations, Hollywood knew where we lived.

The three lectures that I attended at Cambridge were all in the first year. F. R. Leavis had to be experienced once and Hugh Sykes Davies turned out to be the wittiest academic I have ever heard. The third lecture that I sat through was given by the urbane and mannered F. L. Lucas, who began his exposition of tragedy with these words: 'As I was standing on King's bridge this morning, a remark by Schiller flew into my mind, much like the swifts darting across the sky-reflecting waters of the river below…'

Quite. I had found a friend in the mordant John O'Callaghan, breezily enough known to everyone as JOC, who faced down this sort of stuff with an exasperated Irish scowl. He insisted on eating a regular lunch and found a place that suited our pockets, a Greek restaurant in Benet Street. The owner and his daughters were Greek but the menu was an exercise in what you can do with minced lamb using a pastry cutter and a little ingenuity. The chips were excellent.

Moreover, we created a daily *causerie* in which Lenin rubbed shoulders with Shakespeare, and Stanley Matthews jinked his way past Jelly Roll Morton. The number at table varied but seldom fell below four.

JOC was the sanest man I knew. He ran a motor-bike and would go on to teach himself to fly. His rooms were in Trinity's Green Street Hostel and he entranced S by inviting us both to coffee on Sundays, after Mass. We all came from roughly the same background, a source of great reassurance when discussing the future. I can see now that I was admiring something fearless in him, principally an absolute refusal to kiss the flag. His conversation was acerbic and demanding, his essays terse to the point of insult. He had come up in company with another South Londoner, D'Arcy, who played Goldsmith to his Samuel Johnson.

One Sunday, D'Arcy had been left in a bath of cold water for his own good after spending most of the previous night too drunk to stand.

'Isn't that dangerous?' S demanded nervously.

'He's quite used to it,' JOC explained.

All the same, we put down our coffee and looked into the bathroom. D'Arcy lay fully clothed and unconscious, the water lapping at his nostrils, his face a ghastly white.

'I'm not sure this is right, JOC,' S said doubtfully.

'Nice girl,' he commented next day. 'DArcy's indestructible. But she wasn't to know that.'

It would be much easier to evoke Cambridge if I had enjoyed

a closer collegiate life. I joined nothing, supported nothing. John Tydeman, my school fellow in Hertford, was also at Trinity, producing and directing plays; I never saw one of them. The only poet I met was through the Wrestler, who had discovered and encouraged the wonderfully talentless Maurice, recently discharged from Fulbourn Asylum. If the beginnings of the poet's task is an ability to look like one, Maurice had cleared the first hurdle, for he sported a Bill Cody beard and whiskers, and was the only man I have ever met to wear a cloak. His oeuvre was gathered in a collection of Silvine notebooks, the pages glued together by semen and coffee stains.

Maurice haunts me. To this day, every university town has its own version of him: self-taught, blustering, maniacally confident. For a while in later life I lived in the same street as just such a one as he, only this time a painter. Terry once tried to sell me a work depicting a Spitfire flying from a nun's rosy buttocks: Maurice would have loved the conceit. His poems were only intermittently intelligible. Some of them could only be recited and their meaning guessed at when he was in a state of erection. He was born in the wrong country and probably in the wrong century. On his occasional visits to borrow money, he lay on Mrs Wilson's eiderdown, grinning through his whiskers and drinking British sherry from the neck of the bottle.

'I miss all the sane people I knew in the bin,' he confided once. 'It's hard work out here. *You* are hovering on the brink of madness, my darling, and some of your friends are barking. Too many books!'

'Why do you call everybody your darling?'

'It's like a ship's foghorn, announcing my presence,' he replied slyly. 'Toot, toot, is there anyone out there?'

'When did you started writing?'

'I was a child genius,' Maurice explained. 'I alone saw the spangled tights flying like swans in the impossible cosmic circus.'

He really did talk like this. I used to watch him very closely to see whether or not he was sending me up but he was too self-absorbed to waste his gifts on ironies.

'I saw a naked boy today, peering from the top deck of a bus. His eyes beseeched me, his fair locks stood on end! Right there in the street I bared my breast and shouted, "I cannot pay your fare."'

'Was he really naked?'

'There you go again,' he sniggered. 'Asking exactly the wrong question!'

Mrs Wilson took a dim view of these night visits. Maurice had a penchant for opening the window and declaiming to the lighted windows of the houses opposite. It had not gone unnoticed.

'If that friend of yours isn't just some dirty old tramp, I shall want his name and college because the Proctors ought to know about him.'

In the end it was I who was reported to them. On the night of my twenty-first birthday, Maurice and some others gathered at Mrs Wilson's for a drink and poetry reading. One thing led to another and it was proposed we should go out for last orders. I was crowned with a lampshade taken from the ceiling light and we set off for the Baron of Beef. Maurice diverted us into a pub along the way.

It was Mr Wilson's local, where he was a member of the darts team. His wife sat beside him, scowling as ever. It took her a moment or two to recognise the lampshade.

'Let me quell the bile that bails the stumps and smite the ball of fiery anger into the darkening deeps where the lost souls gather,' Maurice suggested. She was having none of it.

'And you, Mr Bienkowski! A foreign gentleman who ought to know better! Hanging about with this riff-raff, disturbing the peace!'

But we had the pub and the landlord on our side, so I drank a last pint with the yellow lampshade at a jaunty angle. Maurice borrowed Mr Wilson's darts and hit the bull's-eye with his very first throw. His second hit the slate and with the third he offered to poke out his eye in contrition.

'You didn't think you were bringing the name of the university into disrepute?' the Proctor asked me two days later.

'I was enjoying a drink with friends.'

'Wearing Mrs Wilson's lampshade.'

'I have offered to buy her a new one.'

'And this poet fellow? Is he published, by the way?'

'The climate is not yet right.'

The Proctor twiddled his pen.

'Mrs Wilson would like to have you flogged round the fleet. Stay out of her local in future. I think in the trade it is called barring. You might wish to buy her a small box of chocolates. And now good day to you.'

S came down most weekends. Next to the Corn Exchange was a pub called the Red Cow, which had rooms of the sort used by commercial travellers and other solitary men, dark and gloomy rooms that smelled of damp wallpaper and flannelette sheets. We lay in bed, shocked at our own depravity, listening to the faintly menacing sound of roller-skating going on across the road in the Exchange. At ten-thirty it ended and the street was quiet, except for the occasional clack of high heels and leather shoes as couples made their way home. Once or twice, these noises would lead right into the building, dwindling as they came upstairs to whispers and stifled laughter. In the morning, there was the brief social agony of an egg and bacon breakfast taken in the pub. It was served by a wearily complaisant woman with impeccable manners.

As soon as we could we would leave, walking out into golden sunlight where serious-minded young men were making their way to visit Monsignor Gilbey at Fisher House in Guildhall Street. This too had been a pub in its day, the Black Swan, but was now converted for use as the site of the University Catholic Chaplaincy. Gilbey was said to be a notorious Tory eccentric as well as a gifted priest. He was also a Trinity man of the old stamp. One of the stories about him was that he always carried eight half-crowns, sifted to ensure that none of them bore the image of that mere woman, Elizabeth II.

Roller-skating on one side, Monsignor Gilbey and his loose change on the other. The Red Cow was a practical solution to our need to be together but had its drawbacks, most of them aesthetic. S had tried visiting me at Mrs Wilson's, where we lay fully clothed on the bed, terrified at the footfalls on the staircase, which might herald either the arrival of the cheery and insouciant Danek Bienkowski with an invitation to listen to his Sidney Bechet recordings, or might equally announce the ghastly and loveless landlady from hell. A cheap room with a sagging mattress was a necessary but dangerous alternative.

We talked. That was not why we went there in the first instance but what I remember most about that first year of our relationship was the chance to talk and think aloud. And did intimacy take place? My lord, it is my client's case that while sleeping like spoons in a drawer embraces one definition of such intimacy, a closeness of mind resulted (whether accidentally or not) that produced wholly moral consequences. As it might be put, if your lordship pleases, 'So soul unto the soul may flow, though it to body first repair.' And is that the whole of your case, Mr Marvell? In essence, my lord, it is.

At the end of the first year, we celebrated a good result in Prelims with tickets to the May Ball, as formal an occasion as either of us had ever attended. That was the wish at any rate, though the evening ended in predictable braying and tomfoolery as the public schoolboys and their totties, big girls with hips like stokers, began jiving and falling flat on their backs, in the way that they believed the dance was meant to be interpreted.

On this same night, Jack Kerouac was wandering America with Neal Cassady, carrying in his rucksack not one but five unpublished novels. Miles Davis had just signed his quintet to Columbia; Picasso was in Cannes being filmed by Clouzot. Mick Jagger was a twelve-year-old schoolboy in Dartford; John Lennon was fifteen and teaching himself blues harmonica. One cannot say that the world of privilege was about to be pulled down (when does *that* ever happen?) but that year's Trinity May Ball may have been the last to be enjoyed in a wholly unironic spirit.

At midnight, we took a punt and poled slowly past King's, champagne cooling on the end of a string. The sky was dark, the waters glassy and there was a scent of blossom and mown lawns, river weeds and boat varnish. Danek, who had attached himself to us, rescued the champagne and popped the cork with an agreeable chuckle. He was on his way to a sporting third and a multimillion-dollar business. He glugged busily.

'Does anyone else want some?' he enquired with trademark innocence.

Chapter Eight

IN THE SECOND YEAR AT TRINITY, I MOVED WITH Danek into a set of rooms in New Court and began to be taught by Theo Redpath, whose mental austerities were offset by the place where we met, a quite magnificent room overlooking New Court on one side and Neville's on the other. I found Redpath refreshingly awesome. While I read to him, he would walk from a trestle table at one window to another forty or more feet away. At these tables he was writing two separate books. I sat in the middle on a little island created by the sofa.

I hardly expected the practised civilities of the tutorial system to be an honest expression of where I stood vis-à-vis Redpath: we might speak as equals under that code but the talent – and application – was all on one side. I very often came to his rooms with the ink still wet on the page. At some of the more absurd remarks I made – say, on Sophoclean tragedy – he would take out a Vick inhaler and push it gently into one nostril with barely concealed despair.

The truth was, I had nothing original to say. At the same time – and I think Redpath knew this only too well – everything I had to say was original in the sense that it was all new-minted. Thinking in the narrow terms demanded by the academic essay was still a complete novelty. When I read in my translation of Sophocles the remark, 'All's well if Apollo is well,' the pen stopped scratching and I tried to imagine exactly what was meant by that and in what tone of voice the line was first delivered. When I raised the question at tutorial, Redpath stared me down with an expressionless gaze, the cogs and gears of his mind momentarily silent.

'Well, of course, in one sense,' I blustered, 'it's just a formal piety, I suppose. Maybe an added grace-note.'

'And in any other sense?'

'It could be an expression of massive doubt and uncertainty.'

A tiny click as a pawl sought the next ratchet. Encouraged, I tried to find an example nearer to home.

'Say, in front of Stalingrad, it's as if everyone's saying it's okay if the Führer says it is. But I should think in front of Stalingrad...'

My voice tailed away. Redpath fumbled for his inhaler and took a toot of menthol. It was the signal to move on.

I did not know it of my tutor – for he never told me – that he had been Wittgenstein's pupil, from whom he may have borrowed his formidable *visage de bois*. Neither did I know nor care what he thought of me as a person. The traffic was all the other way. Put at its simplest, I had never met anyone like him.

I worked alone, sometimes with the exhilaration of a cyclist pelting down the steepest of hills; sometimes stogged for days on end, unable to move at all. There is nothing quite like the melancholy of reading a text and not being able to draw it towards one. In such a mood it was easier to go for a walk or, perhaps more accurately, a shamble. A walk implies fresh air and exercise, some inspiriting effect from trees and sky. I mooched. I sat in forsaken cafés, or stood on bridges gazing down into the water. Trying to please Redpath (an ambition of which he was sublimely unaware: what pleasure could be got from me that was better than a good lunch or browsing for new books?) became the second most important relationship in my life.

The first, we can assume, was with S, hardly more than an hour down the line by express but otherwise as remote, on weekdays, as Tierra del Fuego. George and Vi had installed a phone to help with his Scout work but the effect of its ringing was akin to someone crashing through the bay windows at the end of an SAS rope.

'Now who can that be?' George would ask nervously, just as he did when there was a knock at the door. A phone call from Cambridge would have needed to announce hospitalisation for it to be justified. It was still the age when absence made the heart grow fonder. When S stood on the Cambridge station on Sunday evening and said, 'See you Saturday,' it meant just that. The intervening hours and minutes were not counted off by text messages and cellphone updates, as they might be today. My struggles with divine discontent were very properly undertaken alone, though they sometimes left their trace.

'I have heard the phrase "desperate melancholy" used twice in the same paragraph,' Redpath complained tetchily on one occasion. 'One such attribution would be too many. Unless you have evidence I have yet to see produced.'

There were tea rooms in Trinity Street where once a year he and his formidable mother organised an undergraduate *conversazione*. Each table had a permanent host but every ten minutes the other three undergraduate cake-nibblers would be rotated. I have no idea whether this method of sharing minds is a commonplace of the art of conversation or was a Redpathian invention. It led to some memorable results.

'Why, ma'am,' a bearded young man in a stetson told the venerable Mrs Redpath, 'if ever I get some of the old French ennui – that *cafarde* thing they have over there? – then I get in my car and drive from Houston in Texas to Austin, Texas.'

'And is that a long way?'

'Oh shit,' this youth sighed. 'I can see you don't know Texas.'

'Doesn't the city seal of Houston have a choo-choo for an emblem?' a beautiful girl improvised, filling the sudden silence with lazy aplomb. Mrs Redpath smiled thinly.

'Choo-choo. There's a word I haven't heard for a while.'

The American and I sank a pint as soon as the pubs opened.

'Do these things happen every week?' he demanded, bewildered. He was not a member of any college but had been invited because he had just finished a novel that he was in no mood to discuss. What little he was prepared to say suggested that writing novels was like wrestling alligators: he had come out of the experience savaged, if with all his limbs intact.

'Do you know Andrew Sinclair?' I asked. Sinclair, who was reading History at Trinity, was famous for having published a best-selling novel in his first year.

'Jesus!' the Texan cried. '*That* guy? I would rather go dancing with Ma Redpath!'

A few years ago I went back to Trinity for a wedding. The service was held in the chapel, which in all my three years I never visited. There followed a reception which, to my amazement, was held on the sacred lawns of Neville's Court, in my day a stretch of grass as innocent of footfall as the Great Lawn of Waltham Cross. I can well remember the grass being cut in Neville's Court with anxious care, overseen by the Head Porter but, more importantly, mown by a Fellow of the College in an Aertex shirt and khaki shorts. No mere gardener could be expected to do the work satisfactorily. And now here we were tramping about on it like punters at Towcester racecourse.

The wedding feast was held in Great Hall. I was honoured

to be seated at top table, where, as Master, Lord Adrian had presided over the evening congregation, a remote and august figure flanked by senior Fellows and their distinguished guests. It seemed wrong for me to be sitting there, looking down on seriously foreshortened figures as waiters scurried to and fro among them – and doubly wrong that so many of these college servants were women, a thing unheard of in 1956. The thumb that went into your soup in those days belonged to a decrepit old man whose connections with the job were lifelong. As he worked, it was a point of pride for him to conduct a boisterous conversation with his neighbour in the next aisle, as though serving two or three hundred babbling students at table was no more demanding than feeding pigs.

A woman at this wedding was kind enough to ask me whether I had been lucky enough to go to university. Indeed, I said, and to this very college.

She peered at the ruins of who I now was for the ghost of the undergraduate. Her mind searched for a compliment.

'It must have been very exciting for you to be among so many clever people.'

'Well,' I countered, 'I was so incredibly gifted myself, I can't say that I noticed.'

'Um, should I have heard of you?' she asked doubtfully.

Her instincts were good. For every High Court judge or tottering old diplomat who remembers walking across Great Court in the days of his undergraduate pomp, there are hundreds – indeed, thousands – of college members who honour the place more for its suave manners and undemanding social character. We were clever enough to have got there and, over time, smart enough to know that what we had to offer was, by Trinity's own exacting standards, second-rate.

That was in the nature of things. What looked like easy and sometimes agreeable work had the power to lay you by the heels. I soon discovered that the number of firsts awarded in each part of the English Tripos could be counted on the fingers of two hands. The wedding guest was right in that one respect: I owed my place there to good fortune and learned from it the best lesson of all, that wishes are not horses.

'Do people still climb this tree?' I asked a current student, indicating the one that stands in New Court. He inspected it cautiously.

'Erm, why would they want to do that?'

No more gate money, no more climbing in, no more trouble with gowns or the licensing of bicycles. Happily, the professional sardonicisms of the porters' lodge were still in place. I had arranged for a wedding gift to be left at the lodge and called to double-check that it had been safely delivered.

'We are not postmen, sir,' a porter responded gravely, 'but I believe we can manage a parcel or two when push comes to shove.'

For many peering through the gates of Trinity, Great Court still exhibits a privileged hauteur. But I had the sense of the street having subtly invaded the college since my day.

Everywhere I looked there was change. In the corner of New Court there had once been Victorian baths that filled with brown water announced by thunderous knocking and racking coughs from the pipes. It was wise to stand back: there might be geysers of superheated steam projecting quite sizeable flakes of iron; more commonly the system delivered an apologetic torrent of cold water. This form of Russian roulette was now long gone. In their place were arrangements generally met with in Travelodges or the better sort of seaside boarding houses.

We grammar-school boys hung together for the sharing of common tastes and perceptions. We spoke differently and had great trouble with the offhandedness of the predominant patois, which was all public school. I never met anyone of my own class – with one exception – who was not a little shocked at being there in the first place. It was the greater style to assume, with just the right degree of nonchalance, that if one was going to be anywhere for the next three years, it might as well be Trinity. (And what joy to discover that the Pitt Club, in my day the epicentre of all this insouciance, was now a pizza parlour. It was like being told that King's College Chapel had become a carpet warehouse.)

In this mood, I stared at the blank windows of the college, thinking of my bedder, Mrs C, and her Dickensian monologues.

'I seen the bearded gentleman in G8 this morning, sir, standing in his room stark bollock naked if you understand the expression and reading from a big book. So I says to him, ooh, if you don't remind me of the Lord Jesus Christ, I says. And he gave me a sweet smile that come straight out the Bible.'

'He is in fact reading Theology, Mrs C.'

'And don't I know it. So I finish dusting round him and in I goes to the man he shares with, Mr Phelp, and what do I find but he's asleep in bed with a young lady. Now you know the rules, sir, Mr Babcock would have my guts for garters if I didn't report the pair of them. That's a rustication we're looking at there, plain as can be. So I go back to see what old Jesus might have to say about it and blow me if he hasn't got back into bed hisself.'

She wiped her mouth with the sleeve of her moth-eaten cardigan.

'So now I'm in what you gentlemen call a quandary. I walks all the way down to the pantry and my hands are shaking like this. Babcock's snooping about outside – he's done his knee in again, by the way – and I've got me broom in one hand and Mr Phelp's future in the other.'

'What did you do?'

'I'll tell you what I done. I made two cups of tea and took 'em up on a tray. Knock on Phelpie's door, walk in, all casual, and ask, "perhaps the young lady would like a cup of tea?" And then I goes on, very pointed like, "To *revive* her." She jumps up, hand over her halfpenny, looking for her specs. I would say she was flustered. Two minutes later she's off, blouse hanging out her skirt. I'm just coming in to see to you, Phelp runs down the stairs, gives me a big wet kiss and bungs a pound note into my hand. And that's been my morning.'

Most of the jazz you heard floating from a college window was, in the language the day, trad. Danek, as described, was a Sidney Bechet/Mezz Mezzrow fanatic and would beg me to go with him to the Rex Ballroom to hear students Dick Heckstall-Smith and Derek Amoore recreate that magical combination. The Rex was also on the touring circuit and we were in the raucous crowds losing sweat to bands led by Chris Barber, Ken Colyer, Mick Mulligan and Humphrey Lyttelton. There was something primal about these nights at the Rex that acted as a safety valve. As Danek pointed out, the fans who danced there were running away from *Take Your Pick* and *Dixon of Dock Green* on the television, or hit-list singers like Doris Day and Dickie Valentine. They were the authentic voice of protest.

I was not completely convinced.

'You think George Melly is going to lead the revolution, do you?'

'Not him necessarily,' he answered. 'But something or someone will come along.'

Something did. Poor sheltered fools that we were, we had never heard of Little Richard, Carl Perkins, Gene Vincent or even – in my case – Elvis Presley. There was a man with a gingery beard in New Court who sometimes came with us to the jazz club. One morning we asked him where he had been when he should have been stomping (oh dear!) at the Rex.

'I was at the Cambridge Trades Club,' he answered calmly, 'listening to rock and roll.'

This outrider of what was to come was Gordon Hainsworth, later Chief Education Officer of Manchester. He spoke in the flat tones of his Leeds childhood, where he grew up only a street away from Alan Bennett. Like Bennett he was an historian and had a huge appetite for learning. Nothing about Trinity fazed him for a moment; he was the exception to the idea I had that snotty grammar-school kids were there under sufferance. Under his beard he wore a semi-ironic red bow tie and his glasses had lenses bound by gold wire. He looked the part. Seeing Hainsworth's urgent steps as he pattered back from lectures with four or five books under his arm was what tourists came to Cambridge to witness. For me, additionally, he was the epitome of what could be achieved in the state system of education. He feared no one and was the equal of anybody.

The thing that reminds me most of him now was his rooms. You were not allowed to alter the prescribed colour of the walls and we lived as a consequence in grubby cream interiors, often with the ghosts of picture frames outlined by dust. Gordon got round this by hanging loose wallpaper, the seams secured by sellotape, the top and bottom of each sheet anchored by drawing pins. In his ground-floor rooms we sat in a pine-green cave, lit for drama, drinking very much better wines than were on offer anywhere else. We experimented with clay churchwardens but really this was a place for small cheroots. I drank my first glass of Armagnac here, smoking something pungent from Indonesia.

His adoring girlfriend overtopped him by nearly a foot. With S, we punted out past the open-air bathing station in the summer months, the perfect picnic selected and packed by Gordon. While he poled, his trousers clinging desperately to the chub of his hips, the cuffs of his shirt overreaching his hands, we kept up that particular earnestness that we took for granted in others: a broadly socialist critique of society that had some theoretical base but was largely fuelled by exasperation with the here and now.

There was, for example, a famous story going around Trinity about a candidate for admission who came from a public school. His headmaster had endorsed the application in very succinct terms: 'Mr X has little between his ears but rowed stroke for the school boat. He stands six foot four in his socks.' Come the glorious day, this man – the headmaster – would be led from his study, offered a blindfold and a last cigarette, and then shot against the wall of the fives court. There were those who would extend the same summary justice to the (successful) candidate, now wandering about in shorts that set off his thunder-thighs; and others who wanted to prick the names of certain Fellows of Trinity, whose fascistic absurdities they deplored. But, as we smoked Gauloises and lolled on sun-drenched cushions under a picturesque willow, it was hard not to admit that we too could be seen as beneficiaries of the same shoddy swindle.

'Oh, how d'ye do, don't you know!' anglers would shout sarcastically from the opposite bank as we lazed. Gordon had the edge on them – he was wholly free of the politics of envy and, as he had proved with his tastes in music, knew what was just around the corner for these fat boys and their maggots. It was not Russ Conway.

S (I think) remembers these Cambridge days as halcyon. Such a world as we inhabited at weekends was probably never to come our way again. The very motion of a punt, the speed at which it ambled past the landscape, the intense languor that followed stepping out of it onto warm cobbles when the best of the day was done, were all intoxicating.

I remember the end to one golden afternoon, when a man in a white gown and a solar topi, sporting a biblical grey beard, was addressing a thin crowd from the steps of his motor-home, a converted wartime ambulance. It was dressed over all by texts that announced the coming Armageddon. He was assisted by his daughter, a young woman of overwhelming beauty.

'Do you see what I hold in my hand here?' he cried. 'Many would say, why it is nothing but a stone! But oh, you thoughtless hedonists, you who have chosen the flesh over the spirit! What I have here is a piece of petrified sin from Mount Ararat. Let *it* speak to you, if nothing else will.'

Fresh from a punting picnic, we stood with naked feet,

burnished by sunshine, planning to buy a pint at the Mill the moment it opened. The prophet who had been to Mount Ararat caught my eye, hesitated, and then raised his arms in supplication.

'Help these lost people find themselves!' he bellowed.

Anthony Eden did his best to point the way. How this came about means recapitulating my first year and retelling it in calendar terms. In doing so I am condensing the output of many drunken altercations and the stabbing of a forest of forefingers in late-night sessions that exhibited the peculiar circularity of undergraduate argument. In this light, it is perhaps best to preface what follows by a remark made by a stranger to our drinking club.

'The fact is,' this man said, 'the bastards can do what they like and there's not a thing we can do about it. In twenty years' time, there won't be anything we'll *want* to do about it. We'll be the bastards then.'

In February 1956, Eden and President Eisenhower issued the Washington Declaration, reaffirming joint policy in the Middle East. It was the sort of unexceptional agreement that reinforced to the British public the idea of the special relationship between the two countries that Churchill had worked so hard to promote. Whether this relationship existed in fact was another matter. The world was being managed by two superpowers and Britain, as events were to prove, could be ignored or contradicted as the occasion demanded.

When this declaration was made, Eisenhower had been in post three years; Eden, as leader of the Conservatives after Churchill's resignation, no more than ten months. As Prime Minister, his period of office was even shorter, dating from elections the previous May. He went to America pursued by Churchill's son, Randolph, then a journalist on the *Evening Standard*, a man with a stock of disdain towards his father's successor sufficient for the entire country. Refused an interview with Eden, he set himself the task of being the wasp at his picnic.

Eden badly misjudged his visit to the White House. His task was not to impress the President so much as to convince his Secretary of State, John Foster Dulles, that we were still a nation able to play poker for the highest stakes. He failed. Eisenhower was seeking a second term in November and it was Dulles's job to keep the Oval Office focused. Clearly the Middle East posed huge problems to both countries; but only a fortnight after Eden was received at the White House, a seismic event occurred. In an electrifying speech to the 20th Communist Party Congress, Khrushchev denounced Stalin.

Dulles had a simple formulation for dealing with foreign policy issues: you knew you were making progress if the problem that you had last year was not the same as the one you had today. The denunciation of Stalin was, in poker jargon, a whole new deal. The vacillating and tentative Eden, already in the grip of terminal illness, was not even to be invited to the table in a game like this. As for the joint declaration on the Middle East that he brought back with him, it was repudiated by the Soviets only twelve days later. Any despatch of British or American troops to anywhere in the region would be seen by Russia as a violation of the United Nations Charter.

In April, Bulganin and Khrushchev made a pre-planned ten-day visit to Britain. When they came to Cambridge, their slow-moving cavalcade was met in the street by rowdies singing 'Poor Old Joe'. I was watching from the gates to Sidney Sussex College as they passed and remember the Soviet Premier peering in disbelief at a languid figure wearing white shorts and a sweater knotted around his neck, singing lustily and at the same time exploring the strings to his squash racket with well-manicured hands.

Much of the run-up to Suez took place in the long vacation. Try as they might to like Eden, a mood of exasperation was growing within the Establishment. At the end of August, a month after the seizure of the Suez Canal by Nasser, *The Times* published a leader written by its editor, William Haley. It included this swingeing reproof:

Doubtless it is good to have a flourishing tourist trade, to win Test matches, and to be regaled by pictures of Miss Diana Dors being pushed into a swimming pool. But nations do not live by circuses alone. The people, in their silent way, know this better than the critics. They still want Britain great.

The Times had supported Chamberlain's policy of appease-
ment towards Hitler (an issue over which Eden himself
dramatically resigned). This was new. Were we going to be
pushed around in Egypt or were we going to fight? The silent
people conjured by Haley in his leader included George and
Vi and my father. All three would have felt a righteous indig-
nation that our country was not being treated with the respect
that its position in the world demanded. Who was this horrible man Nasser, if not another jumped-up Hitler?

On the last day of October the RAF began bombing
Egyptian air bases. On 2 November, I joined an anti-war
protest march that was forming up outside the Cambridge
Labour Club. An old man tottered out of the premises,
reversed his walking stick and struck me a nerve-numbing
blow on the arm.

'Not a soldier among you,' he shouted. It was the only
time in my life that I have seen this image worth applying to
another human being: he was beside him with rage. It was
farcical, to be sure; but it was also terrifying.

I had signed a paper petitioning the Government to
abandon its policy and declaring that I would refuse to serve
with the Colours, were I to be recalled. Whatever the old man
meant when he struck me, it came to me that I was not and
never had been a soldier in the way that he had been. He
was too old to have been a veteran of the Western Desert
campaign and his battles were likely to have been fought in
Flanders and France. A refusal to serve then would have

resulted in execution by firing squad at Étaples. But what gave the story its specially hideous shape was not that he had attacked me but that he left the Labour Club to do it.

We set off on our march through Cambridge. Most of the heckling we had came from other students and there were one or two scuffles. It did nothing for my temper that the University Communist Party took the salute, so to speak, from an open-topped Mercedes parked outside the General Post Office. Just as the marchers were dispersing, a soldier in uniform jumped onto a park bench and held up a copy of the *Evening Standard*. The headline read PARATROOPERS TAKE PORT SAID AIRFIELD. It was the signal for a general fracas.

The botched invasion of Suez destroyed Eden, who resigned two and a half months later, in January of the new year. At the university, it was a time of great bitterness. For me personally, it provided the sharpest lesson yet in growing up. I had signed the anti-war petition only with my name and that of my college. A fortnight later my father was interviewed at work by security officers from MI5. As he was someone who had signed the Official Secrets Act and was working on classified projects, they wanted to know what he thought his son was doing.

'I told them you were as dangerous as dog shit,' he said contemptuously.

I had expected him to be far angrier than that.

*

As everybody knows, the Russian tanks went into Budapest less than a week after British paratroopers landed at Port Said. It added to the sense of confusion that had swept over Trinity. On one staircase in Great Court a man framed his Military Cross, won in Korea, and displayed it prominently above his fireplace. His neighbour, from the same school and social background, drove his father's family saloon across Europe, the boot stuffed with medical supplies. The Wrestler and I had written a poor piece for the *Cambridge Reporter* about student reaction to the crisis; for a few days we were chased by a toby jug of a man from King's who wanted to thrash us with a blackthorn stick (a Baden-Powellish detail that lingers).

My vacation job that Christmas was in a public-sector nursing home. There was no doctor in residence and the place was run by a German nurse and a drunk who had been in the RAMC. The rest of the staff was made up of auxiliaries like me. There was more money to be made on night shifts, when the German girl and I sat drinking red wine, flirting and listening to the poor devils who had been dumped in this terrible place to die.

It was the end to a very complicated year of my life. If I was not yet married, nor even engaged, a room in the Red Cow was as binding as a wedding ring, and the key date in my life was September 1958 when, as they say, S and I would walk down the aisle together. Meanwhile, my country had fought an unjust war, I was an unwanted lodger in the family home and – perhaps worst of all – I had already discovered the limits of my academic ability. So far as Cambridge was concerned, I was boxing above my weight. (This realisation came to me when I was actually in the examination halls, writing an essay for Part One of the Tripos. I imagine it happens often enough to candidates. The effect on me was rather like the honking of a very loud motor horn, not from the street outside, but from inside my head.)

Two days before Christmas, I undertook to give an old girl in the nursing home a bath. She was a huge Cockney with layers of fat that rippled like the tide coming in over the sands.

'Now all you got to remember is don't let my back go. If that goes, you'll never get me out the bleedin' bath again.'

I was pondering how to get her into the bath in the first place.

'Garn,' she chided. 'You seen what I got before, I don't doubt, a nice-looking young boy like you.'

'Never arranged in quite this way.'

She yelled with laughter.

'Gawd, if that miserable sod Ernie could see me now.'

I got her into the bath and sat her forward with her head over her balloon belly. And in that way, we talked as I sponged. I told her about S and Trinity, where all the brainboxes lived.

'It don't sound much fun,' she observed. 'Ern, he worked at Covent Garden all his life. Like I told you, he was a miserable git but I think he had more fun than what you're having, you unhappy little basket.'

I pulled her up by her armpits and she suddenly let out a yelp.

'Remember me back! Gawd love us, I told you—'

She reached around my neck with her bolster arms, too late to stop herself being unhinged at the waist. I was dragged into the bath on top of her, my face between her breasts. Birgit, the German nurse, ran in and disentangled us. Ern's widow coughed the water out of her lungs.

'I bet you wished it was her you was on top of,' she said, laughing.

'Now I shall make report about this incident,' Birgit promised. 'I have to do. It is the law.'

'Fuck the law,' the old woman retorted. 'This is England, girl. You ain't in Germany now. You leave well alone.'

I cycled home next morning down empty lanes, thinking about what she'd said. Despite all the ground tremors I had felt that year, no earthquake had taken place. This *was* England. During the night, a plywood reindeer attached to a pub in Cheshunt had lost its footing and was hanging by its back hoofs. The lights that picked out its shape were extinguished but the smile was still there. More of a seasonal grin, perhaps, but worth the effort for all that.

'What's got into you?' my mother asked when I got home, passing me a bacon sandwich.

'Last night I had a bath with one of the patients.'

'Do you know what, Brisie?' she sighed. 'I believe you.'

The radio was on and in the kitchen Doris Day was singing 'Che sarà, sarà'. In Hungary, hundreds, perhaps thousands of young men like me were staring at cement walls covered in blood and excrement, their faces prised apart by shame and despair. My mother was watching me closely.

'You ain't hardly twenty-one and you've bollocksed your life up completely, haven't you?' she said, passing me a Weights. 'You won't get more'n a box of matches from your father this Christmas, after all the trouble you put him through. You know that, do you?'

'Fuck him!' I shouted.

'That's nice,' my mother observed, not without a little secret smile.

The way out was S and her irradiating calm, her unflinching purpose in life that stood as a reproach to my own confusion and self-pity. The road ahead was already paved with her deliverable promises. Why then did I dread taking it?

Chapter Nine

CAMBRIDGE HAD LANDSCAPES FOR EVERY MOOD. Snow along the Backs; the first faint pricking of leaf in spring seen from a library window; the busy hissing of pressure lamps hung above market stalls on Saturdays, the smell of books, the smell of Firework Night. (In 1957 the police attempted to restrain students from climbing lamp-posts by winding sticky tape around the lower reaches of the columns. The tape burned with a grumbling violet flame and sullen clouds of black smoke.) Sometimes winter skies sat like a dome over the city for days, making the gowned students seem like rooks in a field. In summer the tenderest evening sunshine washed over the colleges, casting blue shadows on the lawns.

Having abandoned lectures, I was more or less at sea, a warm and balmy sea that posed no immediate threat unless one began thinking of the depths beneath. I read, I smoked, I met like-minded friends for lunch, or went on pub crawls. Late at night, I listened over and over to the Vic Dickenson

Septet, music and musicianship that, when I hear them today by some twist of radio programming, bounce me straight back to a room, a pen, a sheet of paper and a floor scattered with books like downed moths.

S and I had been to the first night of the Royal Court production of *Look Back in Anger*, a play that seemed to me so completely a text for the times that I was prepared to overlook both the misogyny and the clunk of a blacksmith's anvil hitting one barn-door target after another. What worked was Osborne's flailing energy and it worked all the better for me because it lacked a clear focus.

'Never lend an actor a pencil,' a suave voice murmured as we filed out into a momentarily transfigured Sloane Square.

But Jimmy Porter spoke for our generation: both the anger in his voice and the self-pity. Just before curtain-up, a burly man and his wife who could easily have been Alison's parents accused us of sitting in their seats. I showed him the stubs and he rolled his head like a maddened bear. He was drunk and so, to a lesser extent, was his wife.

'Don't make yourself ridiculous,' she said, leaning over me. 'Just hop off.'

'I don't think it's us that look ridiculous.'

'Educated people might say "It is we",' she corrected icily.

We had the undivided attention of three rows by now. 'We're not shifting.'

'All right, chum,' the man said. 'Okey-dokey. We'll see, shall we?'

The front of house manager was called and we showed the ticket stubs again.

'Bloody man's in our seats,' the theatre-goer insisted. 'Won't budge, impudent little shit.'

We were in his seats but his tickets were for the following evening's performance. He stumbled away, cooed on by that peculiar English disdain that does not have to raise its voice. Then the curtain went up and little by little I saw what I should have said.

'It's not worth bothering about,' S said of the ticket contretemps, when we were on the train going home. 'The poor man was drunk. His lips were blue. I thought she was worse, if anything.'

'They were both middle-class swine.'

'Oh, nonsense,' S scolded. 'You're as middle class now as anyone on this train. You didn't like them because they were rich. Well, all right, I don't know why you didn't like them. But they're not important.'

'They don't represent a ruling class?'

'I couldn't care less,' she said, disengaging her hand from mine and looking out of the window.

'You don't think they are there to stop us, not because they can out-think us but just by their numbers?'

'I think they live miserable rotten lives and have gone to bed tonight unhappy. I'm very glad I'm not them and I can't see what else there is to say.'

'Who do you want to rule you, S?'

'Gordon Hainsworth,' she said instantly. 'And in time he probably will.'

She threw the theatre programme at the empty seat opposite.

'How I hate these pesky trains. I hate them! If you want to do something worth while with your life, as you keep on saying you do, get me off this railway line before I go mad.'

Or did she say that? Were the words left unspoken and did I read them in her eyes, in the way her shoulders rose like a cat's? Or was it in the way she stood with a commuter's weary practice a second or so before the train slowed and drew into Enfield Lock? (A note to social historians: the train carriage was too filthy for her to take off her shoes but she walked the 500 yards or so home in her stockinged feet.)

The Wrestler, who first discovered the hobgoblin poet Maurice Willowes, also championed Colin Wilson, famously known for sleeping rough on Hampstead Heath with the manuscript of *The Outsider* as his pillow. He invited him to Cambridge to talk about his work and we spent an awkward few days in his company. Wilson exceeded even Redpath in magisterial self-possession; I was specially attracted by his ability to eat junk food (at our expense) with the silent and finicky attention of an alderman at the Lord Mayor's Banquet. He said very little that was startling or interesting (even concerning his unashamed enthusiasm for sniffing girls' knickers) though it pleased him to trump our own reading with texts of which we had never heard. During his visit, he put up at the Red Cow, an irony not lost on me.

Wilson's brief stay stirred a puddle that had been forming slowly in my mind: why had I not written anything myself? I kept no notebooks or diaries, even though sharing rooms with a human annotating machine. I wanted to write but in that hour or so after midnight when I was at my most raw I would sit chewing a biro, listening to jazz, my creative self stuck halfway up the wall and looking back at me with an unhelpful passivity. At such times, I suspected that Danek's pleasant habit of summarising film plots and compiling hit lists of music and pretty girls was merely the tip of the iceberg. Was there a novel hidden away in the box that contained his tennis balls, or tucked under his cheerfully dramatic Hawaiian shirts? He disliked pubs, drank very little and did not smoke at all. He was not a playing member of the poker school that moved from room to room and he generally went to bed early. But was he sleeping? Or writing a work of genius under the blankets?

Danek had a scientist's indulgence when it came to literary discussions. He would listen politely to some rambling account of mine touching, say, Dickens, and then remark that he had heard it said that Thackeray was the greater writer.

'Heard? Heard where?'

'I can't remember. I read *Vanity Fair* for fun once. I think it was on holiday in Spain. There was a girl there who knew all about this stuff. Also Polish,' he added helpfully.

The book I most wanted to write was about the difference between companionship and sex, a path that led all the way back to my mother's tragic choice. It might have been different if Peggy had shown any sign of remembering those days with any clarity. She did not. In the cycle of moods that dominated her existence nowadays, neither the prolonged depressions nor the sudden spikes of dementia had a recognisable root. She was as she was, in the way that other people are incurably jolly, or overweight. I wanted her to have a romantic illness, one that would help make sense of my own part in her life. But it began to occur to me that her wartime adventures had been more akin to setting fire to barns and hayricks than to the slaking of any grand passion. What had driven her was not revenge on a loveless marriage, or existentialist angst. It was a disordered mind. Like the woman who is finally tracked down by the police to a barn and an empty can of petrol, her hair crisped by flame, she had no real idea what she had done.

The companionship that I was trying to describe belonged to George and Vi and their imperturbable daughter. I could read them – or thought I could – like a book. It was the obvious solution to my own cabbage-white navigation that I should head for the harbour that their lives seemed to represent. There, the worst of the storm was always beyond the bar. While it might be tedious to live in the shadow of the real world in this way, it had its benefits. I used to watch George plant out his salvias in the pocket-handkerchief front garden and sow his lettuce according to the instructions on the packet. He was not a gardener at all in the sense that my father understood the term. He was simply doing the same as others down the street and at night he slept – I hope he slept – at ease with himself. He had made nothing much of his few square yards of England but he omitted nothing either.

One stumbling block to expressing all this in fiction was the degree course itself. I had spent two years making simple things sound difficult. There was not a text in the syllabus so simply written that I could not turn it upside down and shake it by the ankles until all common meanings rolled away like coins down a gutter. At about the time that Colin Wilson came to Cambridge, I was reading D. H. Lawrence. The first impression that the novels made on me was dismay, not least because his stock was so inflated at that time. I was exhorted to like Lawrence, but his incurable snobbism and what I perceived as his sexual dishonesty repelled me. Only a little intellectual honesty of my own would have led me to say as much and move on. Instead, my essays betrayed a coward's heart. Moreover, I was dipping my pen into soot. What I wrote was blown away by the slightest breeze and did not outlast the week in which it was written.

To distinguish between love and sex was to reveal more than I had it in me to do. At the simplest level, I would have to admit to S how often I had already wandered into the unromantic dark of casual sexual encounters, hoping for nothing more than to hear myself differently described for an hour or so.

Francine was a burly girl from Mauritius who was passing through Cambridge on her way to Paris. That at least was her cover story. Who knew what oceanic currents had brought her to a single room off Mill Road, where the wallpaper held the plaster in place and the stairs were heavy with the stink of cooking oil? She showed me photographs of her father sitting in St Louis, his dinner jacket topped off by a wing collar and an askew bow tie. He was, she explained, a diplomat. Paper streamers littered the table in front of him. A silver cone party hat stood beside a champagne glass.

It was a photograph of Nowhere-Land but then Francine's crabby little top-floor back room, overlooking the asbestos roofing of an engineering company, had no more real geography about it. To creep up to her room was to enter the fog-bound and unsignposted country of the philanderer, where it is always easier to turn back than carry on.

'Now you can say you have made love to a black girl,' she laughed, pretty much as a fairground stallholder passes you a souvenir plaster Alsatian.

'That isn't why I came.'

'Yes! Of course it is!'

It is no use saying now that only emotionally damaged people behave in this way. When I was twenty-one, I did not even have enough self-awareness in me to make the claim.

'Don't feel bad,' Francine said cheerfully. 'You won't remember me.'

She drifted away on the tide, together with the likes of a friend who attended the examination for Part One of Archaeology and Anthropology in a dinner jacket stained with last night's vomit. Asked to classify a boxful of bones, he divided them into three simple categories: very large, medium size, and (his word) titchy. Then he left the examination hall and, three hours later, the university.

My father bought a 1934 Wolseley Hornet for £70 and arrived one day for a visit, completely unannounced. It was the first time he had ever been inside a college and, after chiding me for dressing like a poof, he insisted on a complete tour of Trinity, as though somewhere or other within its walls lay the justification for it being there at all. I think he was looking for the factory hum of machinery or, hidden away on some staircase, men in white overalls with slide rules in their hands. The non-committal silence of the place annoyed him. To be spiteful I showed him briefly into the Wren Library, fast asleep at eleven in the morning.

He refused lunch and left after two hours. It only occurred to me afterwards that he might have been checking up following his visit from MI5. Certainly he read the papers on my desk with far too much casualness and twitched open the single drawer on the pretence of looking for a pipe cleaner. When he was introduced to Danek, his eyes narrowed at once and his chin came up. But his suspicions were blunted by a long exposition from the genial Pole about quantum physics.

'Say, for example, you are playing snooker – it doesn't have to be snooker, it could be tennis – but anyway, the ball, I don't know, rises from the table in some way and circles the room, or if it *was* tennis—'

'That's the ticket,' Bert said absently. 'And your father? Is he political?'

'He imports Polish food,' Danek answered, bemused.

Before he left, my father said a very strange thing. Walking back to the car, which he had left outside Great St Mary's, he pointed to a crowd of students coming back from lectures.

'What you have to get into your head is that any one of these could be the Prime Minister of the future.'

'Or maybe you're talking to him now,' I countered.

'No,' he said. 'You're like your mother. You can't see further than the end of your nose. It takes more.'

He had never read Conrad (come to that, neither had I) but I knew as if struck by a bullet what he meant. He was indicating the horror. He got into the car, which smelled so sweetly of leather and oil, took two clothes-pegs out of his jacket pocket and used them to jam the dashboard throttle open. The Hornet's engine coughed a few times and then caught. I had my hand on the sill of the window. He waved me away impatiently and set off in a plume of exhaust. I had always thought of my father as humourless, but as he went he delivered a sardonic farewell. First the left then the right indicator arm flicked up. He was airborne.

In the summer of 1957 I took a vacation job with Taylor Woodrow, directed there by a management recruitment agency that was, in its entirety, a very large man in a silver-grey suit and lilac shirt. We met in a temporary office above a shop in King's Parade, a good address concealing threadbare arrangements. The recruiter was in his fifties with the genial bulk of certain Italian actors, set off by a fleshy nose and hooded eyelids. His business in life was to be engaging and persuasive, a task that came easily to him. As he explained with disarming frankness, he was here in Cambridge to trawl for graduands who might be the men of courage and enterprise to manage the completely new industry of information technology.

Though he was as English as Cheddar cheese and wore an MCC tie, the one-hour test paper that he set me originated in America. The examination was printed on flimsy salmon-coloured cards that bore the warning not to spindle, fold or mutilate and the questions it set were provided with multiple-choice answers. I was given a special pencil to make my selections. While I worked, on the other side of the desk my friendly examiner studied the Newmarket form and made a few ostentatious notes in a leather and gilt notepad.

I could have told him before we started there was scarcely

anyone in Britain less suited to selling IBM computers. This the results of the test confirmed. On the other hand, they revealed (or so he said) a remarkable topological sense and appreciation of architectural shape I had not known I possessed. It was a lucky finding. It just so happened that the agency had an additional contract with the world-renowned building company Taylor Woodrow, ever on the lookout for smart high-flyers like myself. He need hardly add that we were talking real money. This should have been a warning bell, for surely he could see that I had no idea what real money was. Nevertheless, we shook hands on the deal in the shadow of King's College Chapel and he ambled away to lunch at the Eagle.

So it was that for nearly four months I joined S and my father on the commuter trains into London. To begin with, I was shy of making conversation and would spend the journey itemising what people had in their back gardens and what could be seen of their more intimate lives through thousands of bathroom windows. Nobody so much as glanced back at the passing trains. Occasionally the view would open out a little to reveal a pub where the locals went for a wedding reception or to see Mum off properly once the church service was done and dusted.

There were some in the carriage who never looked up from their books. They read to a backdrop of conversation that was maybe just as lulling as the sound of the wheels on the track. Sally was thinking of jacking it all in and emigrating to New Zealand. Keith was over the worst of his accident and was walking on crutches. The court case came up next month. Old Mr Partridge had been given his retirement clock on Friday and fell dead on Margate beach the following Tuesday. His widow was selling the house and moving to Shoreham. Beryl's baby was so beautiful that she was going to be used in a television ad.

The war, with its richly illustrated stories of loss and separation, was something in the past now, no more than a beach strewn with ancient jetsam. We were in more modern times and the mood on the 7.58 was shyly self-congratulatory. These were the last days of full employment. There was no underclass, no youth culture. Marriage was the outcome to love. Children were the outcome to marriage. There were things to reprehend – London, our destination, was a smoky, filthy old place, for example – but also much to praise.

'I don't know how she does it,' a girl said admiringly of her mother. 'You can put that woman down anywhere, in any city of the land, and within five minutes she knows what shops are worth seeing, where to eat, and what time the last bus runs. Last weekend? We go to Cambridge for the day, she walks straight into a shop and buys just the right tablecloth for Colin's wedding.'

'Cambridge, eh?'

'Oh, we go all over,' she replied airily.

'Did you see inside any of the colleges?' I asked.

Everyone looked up, even the readers.

'We were *shopping*,' the girl explained, as if to Wordsworth's Leech Gatherer.

Taylor Woodrow had its offices in Welbeck Street and I was employed there as a management trainee, under the tutelage of Mr Death, whom I quickly discovered preferred to be called Mr De'ath. I think De'ath had come into Head Office after some years on the road, selling pre-fabricated buildings to emergent African republics. He was a man of very few words. It took him only two days to realise that I was not the man ever likely to sell a West African air vice-marshal hangar space, or a Minister of the Interior a multi-functional conference hall.

Those who did – the company's overseas salesmen – seemed to exist in Graham Greene land, their cables suggesting hardbitten Englishmen living on the last dry land in an otherwise foul moral swamp. The tone of their reports was always wearily upbeat. One advised that Colonel X was out of town but would be back on Friday, in company with his brother-in-law, the Minister for Prisons. Whattime update unnews contractwise. I imagined him brushing fine white mould from his dinner jacket before taking a cab to yet another God-awful nightclub, there to woo the local Tonton Macoute. The salesmen were known about the London office by their first names – Denis and George, Tom and Kim. I never came across anyone who had met them face to face.

De'ath's secretary was a middle-aged woman well used to handling the wrong sort of juniors, who found me filing or indexing jobs to fill my day. I learned the knack of dissembling, coming to work in a King's African Rifles tie and a cheap thornproof suit, yesterday's *Telegraph* (donated by my father) under my arm. I cut my hair short and kept my nose clean, paid rapt attention to internal memos and chuckled sagely at the mild organisational blunders uncovered in the course of the day. (We seemed not to have an IBM computer.)

I had never before worked in an office and the way it influences metabolism fascinated me. At nine every morning, while coats were hung up and covers whipped off typewriters, there was discussion about last night's television and that morning's trains. At ten-thirty tea was brought round and the conversation turned to marital hiccoughs and anecdotes about hospital visiting.

'He looked pale, but then you would. Of course, nosey old me, I had a peep at his chart and was told off by a black nurse. Imagine.'

At eleven-thirty there were announcements about where X was taking lunch, or why Z was skipping it to go to Selfridge's. The afternoon was punctuated halfway through by tea and pieces of Dundee cake, and the working day ended by discussion of what was on television that night. My own metabolism was geared to working until two in the morning, rising at eleven and talking to myself as much as to anybody else. Office life was as novel to me as standing watch on an eighteenth-century frigate.

'Well, I expect it would be different for you,' a plump girl said without rancour but in the most negligent tone of voice. She had married the previous summer and by so doing had won the prize of life. She was like everybody else in Weybridge. Her husband was a quantity surveyor and a little dull when you first met him.

'But a rocket in bed,' she added, her neck reddening at her own candour.

By six in the evening, London had that exhausted feel to it, the air in the streets like one long exhalation. I walked across Cavendish Square much like an actor quitting the theatre after a matinée performance, struggling to find the familiar in myself. Being a management trainee was some days as demanding as walking on as Hamlet. If S and I were not staying on to go to the cinema, I would catch the tube at Oxford Street and read the *Evening Standard* over somebody's shoulder; or study faces that, in the wan and flickering light, might have been sculpted in dust.

I can remember a column inch or so in the *Standard*, about a man in Harlesden who was the proud father of twins. He had buried two bottles of brandy under the apple tree in his garden, against the day his boys would be twenty-one. It was a sign of by how much I had changed that I wondered what made him think he would still be living at the same address. But the other passengers on the tube provided part answer to that: they too – or so it seemed to me – were shack-led to the same job, the same journey home for the rest of their days. Their servitude was not entirely unwilling nor even anything out of the ordinary. I began to look for the man who had buried the brandy. Maybe that white-faced man reading a philatelic magazine; maybe his neighbour with mismatched socks and scuffed Oxford brogues, head thrown back in sleep.

It was the last year or so of monochrome Britain, evoked so often in magazine supplements today as the world we have left behind. There *was* colour but of a muted kind. The management recruiter who had got me into this mess was a daring or reckless man to wear a coloured shirt. On the Central line you could look from one end of the carriage to the other without seeing one. Socks were grey or black, suits suitably drab. Women sat with their hands folded in their laps. Many of them wore gloves. I imagine there were some dubious glances at the character of my green thornproof suit and – a dead giveaway – Hush Puppies.

'You look like a bookie's runner,' Peggy confirmed. 'And where's your braces? Your father's got braces. Where are yours?'

But Bert did not even look up from his dinner. Given the task of ventilating his scratch-built greenhouse before going to school, Neil had forgotten and the tomato plants were struck down by thirst and heat exhaustion. Neil was wisely out of the house, playing cricket with his mates.

The Harlesden hero who had buried the brandy under his

apple tree was due to dig them up again in June 1978. If that
actually came to pass, I wish him well, that man. Like me, he
has lived through some remarkable times and seen the world
turned upside down. I should dearly like to meet his family
on the Central line today. And perhaps I have – was that his
granddaughter with the bare midriff and the tattooed shoulder? Or was his grandson the boy in trainers that cost more
than the old boy had in his Post Office Savings Account the
day he took his spade to the garden lawn?

I was never going to make serious money. S might. They
loved her at the bank and were tempting her to an overseas
posting. Canada had been mentioned. I persuaded my father
to let me keep a month's salary from Taylor Woodrow and one
afternoon we bought an antique engagement ring from a
jeweller's in Wigmore Street. For us both it was a red-letter
day. In a year's time we would be married and – like the girl
from Weybridge – irreproachably our own people.

What S had to offer was constancy. She had the trick of
life that I lacked: she was the same today as she was yesterday
and had made up her mind a long time ago about what was
possible in this world. Her women friends could see this more
clearly than I. One summer Saturday we went to a twenty-
first birthday party thrown by a fey sort of girl who had been
a school chum, at which future young matrons sat in benign
judgement on the hostess, who talked too much, showed her
legs too freely and said ridiculous things. No matter that she

was rich and wore designer clothes, she was just too ditzy to be taken seriously. Her boyfriend was an actor, more specifically a film actor, with a rugged square-jawed look that was already going out of fashion. We spoke a few words, mostly about movies. He had not seen *Wild Strawberries* and did not know the name of its director. On the other hand, he had met Anthony Quayle in the street recently and gone for a drink at the Ritz.

I wondered whether he knew that he and his girl were more pitied than envied by the others in the room. Nobody wanted them to fail (and in fact they lasted). But nobody wanted to be them, either.

'Isn't he *handsome*?' the birthday girl asked. It was like picking a Gold Cup runner by the colour of the jockey's silks.

S's friends Anne and Vic were more reliable witnesses to the way things were. We were going up (or down) on the same escalator. Schmoozing Anthony Quayle at the Ritz might be fun but it was not life. Marriage was life, along with cars a bit more pokey than the '34 Hornet and houses better situated than those in Enfield Lock or Waltham Cross. Nor did you have to be an English graduate to work out what mattered between men and women. I never spoke to Vic about D. H. Lawrence and I may be doing him a disservice now by suggesting that, for him, taking up with a married woman of any kind, let alone someone like Frieda von Richthofen, would have struck him as asking for trouble. Vic had that enviable gift that is missing in every single Lawrentian male: he knew who he was.

Both he and Anne thought that with a bit of tidying up I would do just fine as a young husband. It was vexing that I knew nothing whatever about motor-racing, which happened to be Vic's passion. But the story of how I failed a rainy driving test in the Hornet – largely as a consequence of being unable to close the window on the examiner's side, and explaining to him in too-close detail how, if we did not leave two clothespegs on the choke spindle, we would not get started at all – brought out broad smiles. (When I did pass the test on a second attempt, I drove George's car to a Scout fête, smoking tobacco that he had lent me that bore the innocent brand name, Robin Redbreast. I got out of the reeking Hillman and, the moment I hit the fresh air, fainted. This too went down well. As George himself said, with the gentlest of laughs at my expense, university does not teach you everything.)

I asked for his daughter's hand long after taking the rest of her but there was a point of etiquette in this. It seemed that we could not simply buy an engagement ring and flaunt it about without the formality of trapping her poor father in the parlour and forcing him to turn off the early-evening Western for five minutes. He listened to what I had to say with customary politeness while unconsciously fidgeting to remember how to say the right thing himself. Vi was the amateur actor in the house and would have made a better scene of it. But she was listening behind the door, or perhaps in what she thought of as the prompt corner. What George actually said floored me. He looked up from his armchair with a shy smile and searched for what was in his heart.

'Well,' he murmured. 'Who knows but what you might be able to make something of her?'

If that was to happen, it was not to be out along the Peace River. Vi did not like the idea of Canada, any more than she liked my own vague ideas about taking a second degree in America. We should do what we liked, she asserted, but must expect her to be dead within three months. I owed this shy and insecure woman a great deal but it seemed incredible that she should attempt to blackmail us in this way.

My father had a radically different take on the matter. When I told him I was getting married as soon as I graduated, he stubbed out a freshly lit cigarette and shrugged his heavy shoulders.

'Don't ask me to the wedding,' he warned.

'Why not? I thought you liked her.'

'That's got nothing to do with it. Do you really want to end up like this?' he asked, jerking his chin at the walls, the half-filled ashtray, our pink and yellow coffee mugs.

'I was thinking of something a bit more jaunty, it's true.'

'This America thing,' he went on, implacable. 'If she won't go because of her mother, then show some spine. Go on your own. See something before you leave it too late.'

'The thing is, I love her.'

My father reached for his packet of Senior Service. I had long been fascinated with the unconscious economy employed by serious smokers. Bert searched out a cigarette and lit it as though his hands worked quite independently of his brain. When he noticed that the flame on his lighter was guttering, it seemed to surprise him for a millisecond; but with the same robotic calm he pushed back his chair and went in search of the yellow can of fuel.

'All these books,' he continued from the kitchen, so softly that he might as well have been talking to himself, 'all these must-have things, like the trip to Paris you've been telling your mother about, and still you talk like a bloody shop-girl. If you marry next year, you'll live to regret it. And so will she.'

It was past midnight but the lean-to light was on because that was the way he liked it. It shone on the lawn and the immaculately staked plants, behind which was his tiny greenhouse. At this time of night, freight trains ran into London and one passed now, the couplings snapping bad-temperedly. Upstairs, my mother was in bed and had not been seen for two days. My father stood at the sink, rubbing his eyes.

'What do you want from your life?' he asked.

'I want to be happy.'

'I know you tell people I couldn't care less about you. That's not true. I think about you a lot. But wanting to be happy is such a cissy way of talking. There's only one thing that's going to change your life.'

'And what's that?'

'Work. Putting something into the world that wasn't there before.'

'Having children doesn't count?'

'Any bloody fool can have children. If they want you in America and she's got an offer to go to Canada, what's your answer going to be? If it's "No, we can't upset Vi" then don't come blabbing to me in ten years' time. Either of you.'

'You're saying you really won't come to the wedding?'

'That's right.'

'Is this the sort of advice Jockie gave you when you married Mum?'

He threw his cigarette into the sink.

'I thought with us it'd be different,' he said bleakly, snapping off the lean-to light and lumbering out to lock the door against the night and the inimical dark of human desire.

Chapter Ten

IN MY FINAL YEAR AT TRINITY I WAS GIVEN A
ground-floor room in New Court, next to the gate that leads
to the river. The site was pretty to look at from the outside,
though the room itself had something of the dungeon about
it. To work was to be endlessly distracted by the crunch of feet
on gravel, sometimes a single footfall, sometimes a guided
tour party tramping out to the Backs. In a modest way I was
part of the scenery; more than once visitors stood on tiptoe
to peer over the net curtains into what they imagined to be a
typical student room. They may have been attracted by the
Shelly Manne/André Previn recording of *My Fair Lady*; or,
if they were big band fans, the Stan Kenton Orchestra in
full cry.

It was the last time in my life that I could, if I chose,
spend the day entirely alone. Some people thrive on that; I
did not. The answer to my dismay at how slowly the hours
passed (and what rotten company I was for myself) was to get
up late. In certain weathers, mist would roll in off the Cam

and fill the court with pearly blankness. I grew accustomed to working by crocus-yellow electric light, hunched as close to the gas fire as possible. To sit on the bed in the corner for even a second – say, to retie one's shoelaces – was to give way, throw the feet up despairingly and sleep some more.

'You're in denial,' Gordon Hainsworth explained briskly, the kiss of frost on his cheeks got by marching back from lectures. 'I think you should go out into the fields and howl. You know, tear your hair and roll in the mud. Confess all your sins.'

'In denial about what?'

'You tell me,' he responded, stubbing out his rollie and glancing at his watch. 'I'm off to give Arthur Balfour a damn good thrashing.'

The sombre mood that I brought back from the Cross had one interesting consequence: it enhanced my relationship with the habitually taciturn Dr Redpath. My essays were at long last better written, in the sense of being less prolix, and this new economy of expression left us both with time to kill. One morning, when we had spent what seemed like minutes staring at the Turkish carpet, Redpath astounded me by offering sherry. It was as shocking as if he had undressed completely. While he fussed with the task he had set himself, I asked him the one question that I knew he would refuse to answer.

'Do you think I have a chance of a first?'

'Is that what you want?' he murmured with the greatest

possible delicacy, as of a man passing through a mirror, the better to evade his pursuer. Though I had lost him, I persevered.

'Any chance at all, that is?'

He examined the sherry decanter for a few moments and then bore it away to the side table on which it usually rested. Then he turned and stood with his hands clasped in front of him, almost invisible in the classic gloom of a Cambridge interior. The silence was deafening.

'I must go,' I said, to save him further embarrassment.

S explained that I was suffering from my mother's melancholia, which made me interesting, but enfeebled. It was something to watch out for.

'You don't really sleep all day, do you?'

'No,' I lied.

The news from Enfield Lock was that while George was prepared to contemplate a daughter living in Medicine Hat or Moose Jaw, Vi was as bitterly opposed as she had been when the idea was first broached. We were not going to Canada.

'Whom am I marrying, you or your mother?'

'Don't be ridiculous,' S snapped.

We had long ago given up the Red Cow. On her visits to Cambridge now she lodged with the Babcocks in the Green Street Hostel. The tales that Frank Babcock could tell about me he tried hard to keep to himself. When he worked the porters' night shift, he was notorious for helping young ladies to climb into college over the second gate, assisting them to a more secure foothold by a hand around their ankles and an eye up their skirts.

'Your young man is with a decent crowd,' he told S. 'He's over that gate like a stoat up a drainpipe. Never a moment's trouble.'

The two women frowned.

'What I am trying to say,' he amended hastily, 'is that on the rare occasions—'

'We know what you're trying to say,' his wife remarked sourly. 'And take that bowler hat off my table.'

Babcock eyed me. The minute flickering of his lips, the almost imperceptible pursing they made, welcomed me to the club.

'I suppose now you're going to say you're afraid of being henpecked,' S accused me later as we walked the Backs.

'Nonsense. Ours will be an open marriage, after all.'

'Oh no, it won't,' she promised.

'I hadn't realised that. Anyway, what do you mean, *now* I'm afraid? Am I generally afraid?'

'You're reckless, you always have been.'

'I have had my moments.'

'You can say that again. But it's time to settle down now.'

'You couldn't put that in slightly more attractive terms?'

'No,' she said. 'I couldn't. Besides, I'm sure it's what you want for yourself.'

It was. I had come to depend upon her realism and sang-froid more than I cared to admit. Settling down was a strange way to put it for someone who knew next to nothing about the world but certainly I wanted what S promised about the domestic intimacy that comes with marriage. Recently she had asked me what sort of saucepans I thought we should go for when we had a kitchen to put them in. It was an absent-minded remark and nothing hung upon my reply – or want of it – but the question stuck in my mind. Soon, very soon, we would be boiling potatoes together.

In the second term of that final year I took myself off to the University Appointments Board, a service to students so discreet and low-key that it was housed on a side road on the way to Trumpington. I imagine its real purpose was to advise high-flying scientists about grants and junior fellowships, and to recruit the better sort of chap for the City. It was certainly not set up to cater for those without background. The man whose task it was to advise me was a bleak old fool with just enough background of his own to have secured the job, but with no taste or talent for the work.

'You say you'd like to try broadcasting. Rather ambitious, wouldn't you say?'

'That's why I'm here, to get your opinion.'

'Have you done any student journalism? I believe not. Have you acted or directed? Have you spoken at the Union? Have you – forgive me – joined anything at all in your three years here?'

'I have read English. You can say if you like that I have broadened my mind.'

'Oh, I don't doubt it,' he sniggered, as if I had just pronounced clerk 'clurk'.

Maybe I had caught him on a bad day. Maybe, I thought to myself, he has come into work after a row with Daphne about her obligations in the bedroom, or possibly the amount of sherry she was knocking back while he sat about in an office tricked out to resemble a don's room. Blood was pounding in my ears.

'I'll tell you something,' I said, maddened suddenly. 'I have learned enough to despise people like you.'

He coloured and for a moment or two seemed at a complete loss, as much as if I had struck him. I fell deeper into the hole I had dug for myself.

'I mentioned publishing earlier and you asked me whether I had a family connection to any house you might have heard of. No, I don't. I don't know anyone in broadcasting either. We do have a television. We call it the goggle-box.'

'Lower your voice.'

'I hardly expected *you* to know anything about broadcasting, either. But I won't sit here and be patronised.'

He laughed – or trilled, a sign that he had recovered his composure.

'I meet a man who arrives in my office and rolls a cigarette without paying me the compliment of asking whether he may smoke. He offers as his potential references Dr Redpath, with the important caveat that he has not actually asked that gentleman for permission to use his name. His second referee is an uncle who is not, as it happens, Bishop of Dulwich, but a garage mechanic in Kentish Town. No, let me finish. This student, whom I have never met before, would like, if I understand him right, a place at the top table.'

'Who said anything about that? I'm looking for a creative job, that's all.'

'Yes, but what have you *done* that is in the slightest way creative? That is the point. A good second in Part One of the English Tripos is no doubt very laudable—'

'—we can end this now. I am wasting your time,' I said bitterly.

'I think you are. I will not ask you to apologise for the tone you have used towards me because I sense it is not in you to do that.'

He passed a hand over his thinning hair.

'However. You may wish to walk around the garden for a few moments and recover your composure. Then, if you feel I can be of further help to you, we can try again.'

I walked out through the front door, shaking with shame and embarrassment. There was a satisfyingly deep carpet of fallen leaves to kick and scuff along the pavement. I came to the road where as a boy I had set out for London on a sit-up-and-beg bike. It was galling to admit that I felt no less childish now. I had made a complete fool of myself in front of a man who may not have wished me well but could hardly be said to want to do me active harm. I had played my cards like a fool.

I turned off Trumpington Road to walk across the meadows. The path led towards a bathing station and the children's paddling pool where Figgie and I had once sat with, seemingly, the whole world prised apart for us like an oyster. Six or seven years had completely redescribed this landscape, so that what was magical about it before seemed crabbed and obvious. I walked on down the road to Wimpole. After a mile the pavements gave out and I stumbled along in the gravelly margins of the highway, decorated in one place by a mangled fox. Three miles turned into five. A red sun bobbled over the empty fields. When I saw a bus approaching from the opposite direction I crossed the road and waved furiously.

In fairy tales, the bus stops and I meet the woman who is waiting on the back seat with the sole purpose of changing my life. But in the real world things work out differently. The bus passed without a flicker of interest from the driver; to sharpen the driver's point, it was completely empty. An old man was watching from a cottage garden gate.

'Old car broke down, has'n?' he asked.

'I was looking for a footpath that would get me back into Cambridge.'

'Ah,' he said patiently.

'You don't know of one?'

'What kind of bloody fool would I be if I never, me living here all my years? I can show you a way past Mr Mitchell's farm but that ud be darker than a black man's bollocks by the time you was halfway home. Student, are you?'

'How did you guess?'

'Them shoes,' he replied. 'Come away inside, I'll put the kettle on.'

He was called Bealesy or, if you liked, Old Bealesy. Never married. Lived with his dad, the gaffer, who died in 1949.

'A powerful man for the home-brewing,' he explained briefly.

'Did you ever want to get married?'

'Can't say as I did. I dessay you can't wait.'

'September.'

'Ah well,' he said, polite. 'Now do you know why that bus never stopped for you?'

'I wasn't at a designated bus stop?'

'Because he's a bastard, that old boy. You see a lot, hanging on the gate out there. You should have lived here when the Yanks was here. They'd stop for anyone. Slam the brakes on for any poor bugger.'

'I've just been to an interview about, you know, getting a job,' I said. Bealesy chuckled mightily and clapped me on the shoulder.

'You'm in the wrong place to find one round here, boy.'

*

221

'And what did you get out of the experience?' the Wrestler asked. 'I mean, striding out along the empty road? I only ask because it's something I've thought of doing myself. Tramping.'

'What happened to a career in politics?'

'I would make a better tramp. I have the temperament for it.'

'And the beard.'

'Yes, that too. The unencumbered life. Maybe a poste restante address in Paris. Seen begging in Cologne one month, only to turn up in Mentone the next, smoking a cheap cigar.'

'I was going to ask you: will you be my best man?'

He looked cagey.

'Isn't the wedding day still a long way off?'

'Say no if you're going to be in Cologne.'

'I was hoping you might want to come with me.'

We were in the Maypole, then a quiet pub favoured by porters from Trinity and very unwelcoming to students. I thought of the two of us sitting in a hedge somewhere in a year's time. The image would not steady.

'Ah, there you have it,' I demurred sadly.

'In a nutshell,' the Wrestler agreed.

'Count on me for loose change if I see you selling shoelaces in Oxford Street.'

He laughed. 'I'll probably do exactly what you're going to do. I'll settle for a salary and a pension, a roomful of books and a garden shed.'

'The real world.'

'What is that?' he retorted sharply. 'You might as well believe in the Queen of Timbuktu. You only ever see the real world from a hospital trolley, staring at the ceiling as you say goodbye to the light fittings. No, *not* the real world! I shall live the big lie, like everybody else.'

I persuaded my father that for the final Easter vacation I should not go to work on building sites but spend time in Cheshunt Library, researching and writing a long essay. It was a generous provision from the examiners. A poor essay would be discounted but a good one might weigh with them in deciding between one class of degree and another. For three weeks I sat at a desk with a mound of notes and a very few pages of finished text. I had it in mind to decide what Lawrence meant by what he called 'sex in the head' and in what way (I am vulgarising the argument here in exactly the same terms as I did in that dreadful essay) the loins were a reliable witness to moral truths.

The Cheshunt Public Library was more used to issuing Georgette Heyer novels than finding me a copy of *Fantasia of the Unconscious*, though the assistant librarian, a girl called Katie, rose to the challenge. Across the road was the Lee Valley Growers' Headquarters, a three-storey building that I had helped raise from its foundations, at least to the extent of humping bricks and knocking up cement. One of the labourers on the site was a shortarse whom everybody addressed as

Pimple. He came to see me one day at the library, dressed in his work clothes – a sleeveless Fair Isle pullover and concertina trousers secured by a broad belt.

'I hear you're getting married in September.'

'How d'you hear that?' I asked, amazed.

'Reggie knows someone who knows your father-in-law. What's all this bollocks you're doing here?'

'It's an essay. For the university.'

'What about?'

'Sex.'

'Yeah? And what's your lady friend say about that, then?'

Pimple had so many children that the council had knocked two council houses into one to accommodate, as he put it, the problem that he had with his kipper. He picked up a page of the work in progress and pretended to read it. Something in the way I sat or maybe an anxious expression on my face made him smile.

'Embarrass you, do I?'

I was shocked.

'We're mates,' I said.

'We ain't mates, Brizo. We never was. I see you come in here this morning and I thought I'd wish you all the best, that's all.'

'Well, let's have a drink tonight when you knock off.'

He smiled and scratched the stubble on his cheek and neck.

'I don't think so.'

'Let's go outside for a smoke now. I'll come across the road with you. I'd like to see Chas and Reg again.'

'No, son,' he said. 'I just come to say goodbye.'

It was a blowy day outside, and his hair and the skin on his forearms and chest was coated with cement dust. There was a fresh cut on the muscled meat of his shoulder. He wiped his nose with the heel of his palm, thought about it for a moment and then stuck out his hand.

'Know what your problem is? You want everybody to like you, not just a bit here and there but all the bleeding time. Can't happen. Won't never happen. Even the dopiest kids can work that out. Look after yourself, m'older.'

And then he was gone. He had correctly interpreted to me the fiasco of my interview at the Appointments Board and a hundred other incidents in my life. I stood at the window to watch him cross the road, one hand held up to stop the oncoming traffic, the other hitching his trousers. Reg leaned over the third-floor scaffolding and shouted something, to which he replied with two fingers. He picked up his shovel and began knocking up another load of mortar.

'Who was *that*?' Katie the librarian asked. She knew all about the upcoming wedding and was herself engaged to one Barry, a bit of a ducker and diver whom she had met on holiday in Guernsey. Barry sold carbon paper to impressionable girls like Katie who sat in London offices waiting to be beguiled.

'People will always need carbon paper,' she said, eyeing my essay – in fact, tidying it with her plump little hands. She wore a pink angora sweater and the heat from her chest convected a drift of tiny fibres into the still air. She laughed, as though reading my mind.

'Sex in the head,' she scoffed, quoting the title page.

I used to say, before more subtle ambitions overwhelmed me, that the one thing I was good at was passing exams. I never claimed to do well in them but was seldom bested by the faint air of gloom that they engendered in others.

'You have the God-given ability to put your foot where your mouth is,' Gordon Hainsworth explained. 'That counts for a lot. I can imagine them reading your stuff and thinking, he can't be serious, surely? And then shrugging and pulling the paper off another toffee. Have you asked Redpath whether you can stay on for a Ph.D?'

'I didn't like to be forward, lad.'

'Aye, well, happen you're right.'

'How about you?'

'Me? Not on your nelly. I'm off.'

'Eee, but you'd make a grand doctor, owd lad, you would that.'

'You must come to Leeds one day,' he said witheringly. 'They're ready for you up there. Go to the Vic, behind the Town Hall. They love a cocky southerner taking the piss out of an honest man's accent.'

'What's it all been about, Gordon?' I asked, of our three years at Trinity.

'Fun,' he replied instantly. 'The best fun there is.'

And not a bad valediction at that.

On the last day of examination for Part Two of the English Tripos, John O'Callaghan and I walked outside into dizzying light and ambled towards the Mill. He gave me his gown and, as an afterthought, his pen and a bottle of Quink. Then he stood on the parapet overlooking the river and executed a perfect swallow dive. He swam away towards Trinity, the cheers of the crowd urging him on. For a moment I thought he was in trouble but the turmoil in the water was simply him removing his shoes. And then he swam on. It was an enviably complete and perfect gesture.

Danek was taking his third-class degree and his tennis rackets to Eindhoven, where Philips Research Division was waiting to welcome him with open arms to the world of integrated circuitry. John O'Callaghan had not troubled the Appointments Board and yet had found a place without the slightest difficulty on a trainee journalist scheme. Another friend, Roger Felstead, was joining an advertising agency. I asked him how he had managed that.

'Well, persuasion came into it. And a good suit. Woven by Bullshit & Sons for men with aspiring minds.'

'Did they ask you about the class of degree you were likely to get?'

Felstead laughed.

'They asked me improvise a slogan on bum-paper.'

'What did you come up with?'

'A bloke, say a labourer, is walking towards a builder's cabin. He has a roll of their stuff in his hand. He looks the sort of bloke who nuts you outside the pub. The slogan is: You Big Old Softie.'

'That's brilliant!'

'I'm getting married on it.'

Gordon Hainsworth, the Wrestler and I had all interviewed for teaching posts in schools. Mine took place in Shrewsbury. I had already asked S whether she wanted us to make a lot of money or live in some nice places. Nice places won.

'Oh, we know Shrewsbury,' Vi exclaimed, delighted. 'You've got the River Severn there and everything. It's not more than three hours by car.'

We spent the last days at Cambridge in elegiac mood, playing cricket, having the exasperated Danek coach us in tennis, scratch-building balsa-wood gliders, fishing (and swimming) in Byron's Pool. When I tried to get rid of my infamous dinner jacket at a pawnbroker's, the manager suggested that I donate it to persons interested in amateur theatricals. I chucked it in a wire bin outside the shop.

It was still there five days later.

'It's just, I don't know, so obvious to go back to where I started,' I told S, when talking about what was waiting in the wings in sunny Shropshire.

'But when you were offered the job, you accepted.'

'Yes.'

'Nobody pushed you into being a schoolteacher?'

'Not exactly.'

She knew where this was going. We had been looking in the small ads of the *Shrewsbury Advertiser* for a furnished flat. She refolded the paper with dreadful deliberation.

'It's too late to turn back now.'

'I know that. And I want to get married. I want us to find the perfect flat. I want all the things you want. But I'm edgy.'

'You don't know what love is,' she said, biting her lip in anger.

'I don't know who *I* am,' I countered.

'Ye gods, we're not going to hear that for the rest of our lives, are we?'

'You don't think it's a common enough affliction?'

'What? Not knowing who you are, or talking about it all the time? Look, nobody expects you to be perfect, except your father. It's time to move on. You're what I want and that ought to be enough.'

'You mean that?'

She slapped the grass that we were sitting on with real impatience.

'What do you think all this has been about? I don't care if I never see another damn punt for the rest of my life. You came here to do your best and it worked out fine. Can we please stop looking at things as though life's something you only read about in books? In three months' time we'll be married, you'll be teaching and everything else will fall into place.'

'You're right,' I said, kissing her.

Punts poled past and martins skimmed. From their vantage point on Clare Bridge, a man, his young wife and his family included us in that wide-angle vision day visitors to Cambridge have. We were part of the scenery, two dots on the photograph that his wife took; dots that reinforced the meaning of other dots, walking, lounging, perking puntpoles at the empty sky.

My father, who had never wanted me to go to Cambridge in the first place, was only too willing to bring me away. I stacked my stuff just inside the door, the books secured with jumble-sale ties. My bedder, Mrs C, had been to Walton on the Naze for the day and brought me back a wedding present in the form of two tubby sailors with holes drilled in their caps. One was for salt and the other pepper.

'She's a very nice girl, so look after her,' she said when I kissed her powdery cheek. 'My husband said, he said, well, what's *he* like? And so I tells him – and don't take offence – he's a comical bugger in his own quiet way. Be happy, now,' she chided.

Just before my father was due to arrive, there was a knock at the door. I opened it to find Figgie, standing beside a pushchair.

'How did you know where to find me?' I asked, amazed.

'That's what porters' lodges are for.'

'But I'm leaving today.'

'I knew that too,' she whispered.

We kissed, either side of the baby's pushchair.

'You couldn't have got in touch earlier?'

She nodded downwards at her son, huge tears in her eyes.

'I came to say goodbye.'

I made her walk with me along the Backs and then past the Mill. We sat with our arms around each other on a bench that looked towards a row of willows. In his chair, the child banged a wand of grass up and down.

'Why are we here?' she asked, with the same sardonic smile that had lit my life seven years earlier.

'You know I'm getting married in the autumn?'

'You should never answer a question with another question.'

She kissed me lightly on the lips.

'I go to evening classes,' she explained absently.

'*Did* you know?'

She shook her head.

'No. But that's what happens. People do, don't they? I just wanted to see you one more time. Or for old times' sake or something. Or to get it all out of my system.'

'You said something about evening classes.'

'Badminton,' she said. 'But I have done literature.'

We kissed for the last time and she walked away quite briskly without turning back. The baby's arm waved goodbye, his fist still clutching the stem of grass.

Chapter Eleven

THAT SUMMER, THE SUMMER BEFORE THE WEDDING, I worked in the carnation sheds of a local nursery. We clocked on at five in the morning to cut blooms for despatch to Covent Garden. They were carried up to London in narrow steel vases, four dozen to each vase. If I had searched the length and breadth of the land I could not have found a better way to forget Cambridge and all its joys and woes. After two hours of frantic cutting, we would sit against the wall of the greenhouse and, like horses, smell the water in the vases just as keenly as the scent of the carnations.

The charge hand was a pleasant bloke who had negotiated a twelve-hour day and, when he learned I was earning to get married, wangled me an extra two hours cutting nettles. I did this work with a lugubrious and tetchy Pole who seemed to have been born with a scythe in his hand. He was in love with the teenage girl on our crew and was bemused by her clumsy rebuffs.

'I got money saved, I got my own caravan, she don't want

to know. I'm not asking sleep with me please, I'm asking marry me.'

'She might be a bit young,' I suggested.

'It's because I'm Polish. And this,' he added, pointing to his sparse red hair.

Colin, the charge hand, managed this situation with great skill.

'He really does love her, you know. And she ought to be more grateful, a kid her age. But she doesn't have the language.'

'You think that's the key?'

He smiled.

'And you a graduate,' he chided. 'What's it feel like, having a degree?'

'I can hardly ride my bike home from here at night for excitement.'

'I thought it would be something like that,' he agreed. 'Bit like being a love god, which is my story, since you don't ask.'

Beryl, the teenager, came from a large family, all of them employed in the nurseries. She came to work in a faded cotton frock and what used to be called daps on her feet – black elasticated slippers worn by children for PE. Some days she sported a necklace of lovebites.

'All men is after is to get into your knickers,' she wailed. 'It's like, oh Beryl, would you like a run down to Ware? As if we'd ever get that far. And I say yes, on'y not in some builder's van I wouldn't. Not with my feet stuck in your sandwich crusts and dirty old vests which is all over the floor.'

'Marry me,' Joseph the Pole cried. 'I buy you car.'

'Marry you and have my father come after us both with a shotgun, yes, that's very like.'

The greenhouse was shaded with whitewash and the carnations grew in beds of gravel, fed hydroponically by a time-switch. Once the blooms had been cut for market, we spent the rest of the day budding out, calling and chattering to each other the length of the shed. Colin sometimes organised an impromptu quiz.

'Now here's one for you, Joseph. Who got shot in Sarajevo in 1914?'

'Mickey Mouse!' he would shout from the bottom of the sheds. '"Here's one for you, here's one for you!" You think I don't know no English questions?'

'Ooh, the temper on you,' Beryl would shout back. 'Yesterday, did you know who Dickie Valentine was? No, you never.'

'Bloody fucking Dickie Valentine,' Joseph exploded, before firing off volleys of Polish for minutes on end. Beryl, the minx, would smile secretly, her frock clinging to her thighs with sweat.

We ate lunch at twelve. Colin's sandwiches were beautifully wrapped in silver foil. Joseph's tack was a hunk of bread and sometimes a handful of plums. Once he'd eaten he would roll Beryl a cigarette and pass it to her. She always accepted. Nor did she ever draw attention to the poverty of his lunch.

The easiest topic of conversation was my upcoming nuptials, as Colin called them.

'Now where will the reception be held, I wonder?'

The answer to that was easy. One Saturday, S and I had seen a car with white ribbons drive past in the opposite direction. I made an emergency U-turn and we followed the bride and groom to a community hall in Enfield. Trying to find the caretaker, we were drawn into a couple of drinks with the wedding guests. We made the booking just before people sat down for the catered breakfast.

'Is it nice there?' Beryl wanted to know.

'Seems okay.'

'I shall want something a bit better.'

'Where do you fancy?' Colin asked.

'A castle, or somewhere like that.'

I studied her covertly: she was entirely serious.

The truth was, the wedding was the biggest thing George and Vi had ever tackled. There was a wartime photograph of George standing in uniform on the main square in Brussels, in the middle of a world war but looking a great deal less anxious than he did now. Vi was gay, intermittently, but only in the way that women who are going to have both legs off in the morning put a brave face on things. Neither of them drank and the limits of their socialising were little annual dinners with the Scouts. A wedding was just too vast a concept. To S's great irritation, they put themselves entirely in her hands.

'What about your parents?' Colin asked.

'Twice as useless.'

'Your father turning up?'

'He'd better. I've always wanted to kill him and if he doesn't, this is as good an excuse as any.'

'Well, it all sounds very stylish.'

'You see, I think Beryl's wedding, if it ever happens, will be a whole lot more lively. Where was yours incidentally?'

'Waltham Abbey.'

I thought he was joking.

'We are altogether a better class of people,' he said gravely.

'I shall miss you, Colin.'

'I'm trying hard not to shed a tear myself. One thing's certain, you won't be meeting too many people like us from now on. Everyone'll look like you, or a version of you. Your rambling days are done, partner. No more tumbling tumbleweed for you.'

'That doesn't have to happen.'

'It's called the class system, comrade. I asked Beryl what she thought about you. He's all right, she said, but he talks funny. He doesn't mean to get on your wick, but he does. Well, I said, that's education for you.'

'Do you think Joseph's got a chance with her, when she grows up a bit?'

'That's what I'm trying to tell you,' he said with the kindliest of smiles. 'You're never going to find out. You have joined the ranks of the largely indifferent.'

'Who are you marrying, me or Colin?' S asked that night. She had neither the time nor the patience to listen to tales from the carnation shed. George and Vi were in bed, leaving us in possession of the living room. I watched S iron the straps to her bra and fold her blouses neatly on the end of the ironing board.

'I talk too much,' I confessed. 'But what he said, about the ranks of the indifferent, gave me a jolt.'

The room was scented with the attractive smell of ironed cotton. S stopped what she was doing as a far more practical matter suddenly occurred to her.

'Did you remember to make a list of all those who've accepted on your side of the family? The wedding invitations.'

'I gave it to you yesterday.'

'That's right, you did,' she admitted, after a moment. She studied me from behind the ironing board. 'I shouldn't worry about losing touch with other people, if that's what he meant. A person's only got to say hello for you to go weak at the knees. Isn't that true?'

'It was true,' I said gallantly. 'But that was then and this is now.'

'I should blessed well hope so.'

I finished at the nursery on the Thursday. Two days later, the day of the wedding, the Wrestler sat on the toilet seat, watching me slop about in the bath.

'I can get you out of this, you know. It's the conventional thing to say but I really mean it.'

'I love her,' I protested.

He nodded and stood on tiptoe to look out of the bathroom's vent window.

'Your parents are raving mad. I hadn't realised that. He's out there in the greenhouse, fiddling about with something – no, I can see what he's doing – he's balling twine! Your mother's sitting in the front room thinking of ways to burn the house down. You should write about them.'

'Do you remember the novel you began when we were about twelve?'

'If you really love her,' the Wrestler said, 'then your ship has come into harbour. I shall say as much in my speech. But to answer your question, yes, I do remember the stuff I wrote then. In fact, I brought it with me today.'

He reached into the bath and pulled me up by my wrists. 'Only kidding.'

At the wedding reception, while George was being served his banana surprise by a vexed waitress, it fell off the plate and began sliding down his shoulder. With incomparable grace, he plucked open the breast pocket to his new suit with a crooked finger and it crept inside. It was the epitome of what married men can do when under fire. When he caught my eye, he shrugged and gave me his shy smile.

Aunt Rose was one of the guests on the bridegroom's side. Rose Riach had been my grandmother's best pal in the balmy days at the turn of the century. Two world wars and the threat of nuclear extinction, all as seen from the Borough Road, had left her incurably merry. When we embraced, her stays creaked like ship's rigging.

'What a lovely girl she is,' Rose said of S. 'You bloody Thompsons know how to pick 'em. For looks at any rate. My gawd, but your gran would be happy to see you now and that's no lie.'

'I'm glad you came, Aunt Rose.'

'Jim come all the way across the river to pick me up.'

Uncle Jim, with his incomparable feeling for what was right, had found me a surrogate grandparent, someone from the wicked uproarious past to which I could never return. When I kissed her, she seized my arm.

'Now listen. Your father's a clever sod, no doubt about that, but he can't lay a glove on you in the brains department. Remember that. It's all coming your way, Bri, I can feel it in me water. There was something else I had to say – what was it now? Oh yes, I know. Where's Shrewsbury?'

The day after the wedding we were there. S was right: it was a strange and somehow awesome thing to be married. Our first shared duty was to face down the ghastly old hag who rented us the flat. She lived downstairs in faded but noisy glory. Even on that first Sunday she darted up the broad staircase more than once to oversee our unpacking. Perhaps someone thirty years earlier had told her she was fey and insouciant. There was a husband, although we never saw him until it was time to reverse the Rover down the drive and take her to the pub, which was just around the corner. Nobody of her station in life would ever expect to arrive at a public house on foot.

'Imagine waking up next to her every morning,' I said with perhaps just a touch too much lubricity as we watched her stagger out to the car on ridiculous heels.

'She's old,' S reproached. 'Leave her to me.'

The landlady was perhaps twenty-five years older than us. That put her marriage some time around the year we had been born. But we were young and she was old; nobody dressed like her any longer, or affected her mannered way of speaking. The flat was furnished in a style now seen only in the sleepier country hotels and we heaped particular derision on the presence of what she called a newspaper tidy.

'That is,' she fluted the length of her nose, 'if you intend to take a daily paper. We read the *Telegraph* ourselves.'

It was all absurd and very faintly demeaning but, as S pointed out, it was temporary. Who cared about other people's foibles and frailties? We were one day into the new world, much like emigrants from the old country standing on the dock with only our brains and our passions for company – and everything before us.

'Aren't you going to wear pyjamas?' S asked, as we got ready for bed.

'Until a month ago I had never even owned a pair of pyjamas.'

'But you have some now. I think you should.'

Next morning, I pulled on my bobbly new sports jacket, hitched up my brown corduroy trousers, hefted my briefcase with the brass lock under my arm, kissed the wife goodbye and, so disguised, set off to the local grammar school. As I drew nearer, the pavement became cluttered with other new boys, distinguishable by their caps and empty satchels, shiny shoes and recent haircuts. We walked through the gates together until the point came where I walked on alone, entering the school by a scuffed green door and tramping up some worn steps to the staff room. It was nerve-racking; but, according to the missus, we would be having sausages for tea.

An Afterword

WHEN I MENTIONED THE WRITING OF THIS BOOK TO a man who would like to be described as literary, he smiled, looked into his wineglass with the special condescension that fuels drinks parties and murmured, 'Ah, yes, throwing light onto the dark decade.' I have learned something from life and did not knock him to the carpet. Instead I answered with the snuffling chuckle that indicates (in circumstances like this) submission to a higher wit. After he had sloped off in his white suit and viridian-green shirt, giving his arm to what appeared to be a half-naked child who had been too long at the dressing-up box, I made some enquiries.

He was born the year my story ends. His father (I have to remind myself here that I'm talking about a man my own age) doubtless had a position to keep up when he was young. In the dark decade to which the son referred, this meant an obedience to certain class codes and the persistent disguise of fairly modest social ambitions. In those days it did not do to tip your hand. Deprecation was the right conversational

242

mode; when congratulated on the acquisition of a new and more powerful car, for example, it was the thing to murmur with a wry smile, 'Yes, but it's an absolute glutton for petrol.' Compliments on a recent promotion were best acknowledged by a sigh and 'I suppose they picked the bloke with the broadest shoulders.'

Teaching at a country grammar school fell well within these bounds. We were thirty in the staff room, which was maintained in conditions of abject squalor, exercise books toppling onto copies of the *Daily Mail*, rugby balls skittering about under the table, old clothes and broken umbrellas hanging like felons on the inadequate number of hooks. Make of this what you will but the most searched-for item was a pint bottle of red ink. A little was decanted into a handy coffee cup and then drawn up into a fountain pen, the nib bristling with anticipatory sarcasms.

The door to this hell-hole had a notice pinned to it, reading KNOCK AND WAIT, the title to the first television play I ever wrote. Once through the door on the school side, we were, just as Colin had predicted, caricatures of middle-class twerps, identifiable at a hundred paces by our genteel shabbiness. Walking about the town, even without our gowns, we could be taken for nothing else but chalkies. No amount of ingenuity could disguise us, neither Kitchener-size moustaches nor Lenin beards, sandals in winter or coloured waistcoats on the hottest days of the year.

That the critic I met at the drinks party would one day

waltz about London, knocking fifty and still unmarried, would have astonished me then. The white suit and the green shirt would have seemed to me the equivalent of a leper's bell. Although trilbies – and hats of all kinds – were on their way out, no chap who had his position to think about would dream of going to work without a tie, or in yellow socks, or (in our trade) the wrong *sort* of sports jacket. Even away from prying eyes – say, up a Scottish glen or on a beach holiday in foreign parts – no one of our kind would consider for a moment wearing clothes with wording on them. Nor did we expect to find displays of jocularity written on the chests of young women met with along the way. Fun, as it extended to colours or the length of skirts, would have seemed to us no joke at all. In fact, fun generally was, in a useful phrase, a dicey business.

The trick was to act modestly, at work and in the home. Loud people existed – of course they did – and few pubs were without a boisterous resident drunk. But the majority of men in that staff room were cautious and prudential. Certainly in those dark days there was smoking: in the street, on buses and in underground carriages, in cinemas, and at weddings, christenings and funerals. Smoking was the punctuation to social intercourse. Even among trivial smokers, a suitable Christmas present might be a cigarette box, or what was called a table lighter – something large enough to be crammed into the definition of ornament. 'Do smoke,' the best hostesses would adjure, even at the dinner table.

My contemporary, the cautious father of the flamboyant son, would doubtless have watched *Sunday Night at the Palladium*, hosted by Tommy Trinder. He might have found pleasure in *Double Your Money*, compèred by that fanatical gurner Hughie Green, or enjoyed (as did my own father) *What's My Line?* Bert liked to hate Gilbert Harding, the lowering and testily abrupt panellist, while at the same time admiring what he perceived as his man o' the people directness.

'So you do like some queers?' I asked him once.

'Don't be so bloody ridiculous,' he snapped, the lucky innocent. In tune with the times, he measured sexual orientation by dress. Harding looked so profoundly ordinary and had such a grumpy moustache that he could not possibly be other than straight.

Back to the son, in his white linen suit, his Italian shoes and his stick-thin girlfriend. The terms change dramatically; it is no longer a matter of keeping up a position, as it was for us. The question now is subtler: where to take a position or, better still, how to position oneself to maximum advantage. The certainties that his father could be relied upon to call out at times of national crisis, which dominated his view of politics and literature, history and whatever was valuable in the lives of others as recorded in the obituary pages of *The Times*, mean little to the son. They have all gone the way of table lighters. The word that fills all *his* conversation about life and work is 'opportunity'. As the girl on his arm will soon enough realise, to seize the day means having both hands free. Her lover, or mentor, or however he describes himself, is a man who travels light.

Like me, he has been to university. For all I know, he hated his dad and his old dad hated him. Maybe, too, his first love was someone like S. But marriage is such an old-hat concept these days. At the wedding in Trinity, described earlier in this book, a boy of about twenty-five grabbed me by the shoulders and shouted in my face, 'I intend to spend my life collecting old wine and young girls. What do you think?'

'I think you should choose.'

'Choose?'

'Taking into account your physical desirability, it comes down to a question of cost analysis.'

But of course you cannot insult or deride clowns like these. They understand what I do not: that it is all a question of careful positioning. You can be who you like; the trick is to have enough identities to meet each occasion. There is no one answer.

The dark decade ended where this book finishes. There *were* sausages for tea and for a time I *did* emulate Andrew Wilkinson, who taught me far more about the possibilities of married life – in one rainy afternoon – than the combined efforts of my benighted parents. I kept up a position as best I could and turned for a while into just the prig that the teenage Beryl shied from in the echoing carnation sheds. I fumigated people's sitting rooms with pipe-smoke, looked for insult where there was none, laughed immoderately at my own jokes. After only a few months of marriage and the marking of exercise books, it never occurred to me that I could be anyone other than who I was.